T0067203

Coo'ee

Kimberley Stone

BALBOA.
PRESS

A DIVISION OF HAY HOUSE

Scripture quotations marked (NIV) are taken from the Holy Bible, New International Version®, NIV®. Copyright © 1973, 1978, 1984, 2011 by Biblica, Inc.™ Used by permission of Zondervan. All rights reserved worldwide. www. zondervan.com The "NIV" and "New International Version" are trademarks registered in the United States Patent and Trademark Office by Biblica, Inc.™

Balboa Press books may be ordered through booksellers or by contacting:

Balboa Press
A Division of Hay House
1663 Liberty Drive
Bloomington, IN 47403
www.balboapress.com
1 (877) 407-4847

Because of the dynamic nature of the Internet, any web addresses or links contained in this book may have changed since publication and may no longer be valid. The views expressed in this work are solely those of the author and do not necessarily reflect the views of the publisher, and the publisher hereby disclaims any responsibility for them.

The author of this book does not dispense medical advice or prescribe the use of any technique as a form of treatment for physical, emotional, or medical problems without the advice of a physician, either directly or indirectly. The intent of the author is only to offer information of a general nature to help you in your quest for emotional and spiritual well-being. In the event you use any of the information in this book for yourself, which is your constitutional right, the author and the publisher assume no responsibility for your actions.

Any people depicted in stock imagery provided by Thinkstock are models, and such images are being used for illustrative purposes only.
Certain stock imagery © Thinkstock.

Print information available on the last page.

ISBN: 978-1-5043-7407-1 (sc)
ISBN: 978-1-5043-7408-8 (e)

Balboa Press rev. date: 06/21/2017

In a world soaked in adrenalin, fear and stress, Coo'ee is a gentle reminder that there is a different way to live that will result in more happiness, less stress and fear and with the added bonus of peace and mind. We have not only forgotten that such a life is possible but lost belief that it is attainable. LOVE is calling us to re-discover the way that we once knew and then strayed from. It is imperative that we do. The world is clueless about how to solve the problems that are facing mankind today. God has the answers. God is the answer. LOVE never forsook or abandoned us but we have forsaken and abandoned LOVE as we sought for salvation through technology and electronics. Indeed, the greatest need of and greatest hunger in the hearts of mankind in the 21st century is to do as the Prodigal Son did – come to our senses and return to the Father who loves us.

DEDICATION

This book is dedicated to ALL those magical, wonderful people who have made the transition and gone Home and who were and still are a part of my life: family, friends, teachers, colleagues and neighbors, my brothers Bill and Raymond, my grandmother Eileen Walker, my mother Gwen and my dad Reg. Always loved – never forgotten. I also dedicate this book to my dear friend Anastasia Long, my "wanderlust" aunt Veronica and all my precious friends and family who are still on the earth plane and who make my life immensely interesting and blessed. The dedication is also to the Westward-Ho group in Port Elizabeth – Sheila, Peggy, Judith, Jean, Dorothy, Patricia, Lesley, Naomi, Darian, Maureen C and Maureen N. What a privilege to call you my Velcro Sisters! A bouquet of gratitude also to: Diane Field, Rosemary Halgreen-Visser, Colin and Carol Walton, Sheila Forrest, Ann Schutte, Pat Tee, Esme Brown and the Kimberley Weir family for their friendship.

ACKNOWLEDGEMENTS

My grandmother and my mother were the only people I heard use the word, "Coo'ee". It sounds quaint now, but, the word mesmerized me. I had never heard it before and seldom since. Gran Eileen would call out, "Coo'ee" whenever she knocked on the front door of our house and before she entered. My mother, Gwen, called out, "Coo'ee Eileen" one day as she was passing the room I was renting in Beaconsfield, Kimberley. I can still hear her calling "Coo'ee Eileen!" today! I owe the gift of Coo'ee to them.

I also wish to thank my long-suffering and patient friend, Anastasia Long. I have yet to meet anyone more emotionally stable and mature! Anastasia is the type of person who enriches you in every way just by being in her presence. She always said to me, "You should write a book". Now I have.

Scripture was sourced from: The Revised Standard Version of the Holy Bible and published by Williams Collins Sons & Co., Ltd. Published in New York, London, Glasgow, Toronto, Sydney, and Auckland, printed in Great Britain and also from The Holy Bible – New International Version

EXPLANATION

I have used the words: God, the Beloved, Creator, LOVE, the Almighty etc.in order to avoid overusing one word in reference to God. LOVE best describes God. I have also employed the pronoun" he" as much as possible rather than s/he. The aim is solely to express myself simply and clearly and doesn't, in any manner, imply gender preference.

CONTENTS

CHAPTER ONE

COO'EE

Coo'ee is an old-fashion word, seldom heard today. Pity! Coo'ee is so much better than "Hi", "What's Up?" "Well?" and "Yo!" Even truncated, unimaginative greetings are better than being met with a scowl, grunt or the blank stare that is so prevalent these days.

Why is the world barbaric? A barbarian is a wild, uncultured person in language and behavior. Behavior has become coarse, vulgar, and abrasive and we encounter it everywhere. Is the 21st century refined, gentle and enlightened? You be the judge. It is a common sight nowadays to see the elderly, aged, fragile, feeble and handicapped jostled to the side-lines as younger, fitter people surge forward as a bus comes to a halt. They scramble on board in order to occupy the best seats. How many people say "Please" and "Thank You"? Aren't you fed-up with having your change dumped into your hand when you pay at a check-out? You might as well be invisible! What is the root cause of this type of barbarism? Modern man declared God dead, set himself free from the "archaic" belief in a Supreme Being and became barbaric! When we lose respect for God, we lose respect for everything and the resultant demise of respect has resulted in the disinclination to assume personal responsibility.

Let's consider the two enchanting words of Coo and Coo'ee. A coo is the soft, murmuring sound of doves. It also means to talk or utter something in a soft and amorous (loving) voice. Coo'ee was used as a long-distance signal sound originally used by the Aborigines in Australia and later adopted by others. This is how I believe LOVE communicates with us.

God has never stopped communicating. Since He created, He communicated. It is we who no longer expect to hear from Him. If The Beloved is dead – non-existent, why talk to Him or expect an answer? It doesn't make sense, does it? But, is the world making sense? Are the world leaders making sense? Does it make sense that some sportsmen/women and entertainers are paid obscene amounts of money while teachers, nurses and other vital service providers are paid a pittance? Professional sportsmen/women and entertainers are excessively paid because they distract us from the dire state the world is in. Alcohol and drugs are a central part of modern entertainment and assist in inducing mass amnesia of personal and global troubles. The world descends deeper and deeper into the mire of global strife/confusion whilst populations continue to party at modern-day Roman circuses of mass entertainment! Does it make sense that a murderer's rights are enshrined and enforced whilst the victim has none at all! God help us if this makes sense! The 21st century is no rose garden. The alarm clock is ringing loud and clear. Coo'ee - it's time to wake-up!

The Almighty is calling. I don't know who or what God is - how can I? My mind is finite. How can a finite mind encompass and comprehend The Beloved - the Infinite? I DON'T believe God is a super-magnified human being or a gender. Is God energy? I don't know. I am told God is Spirit but I am incapable of comprehending that too. Whatever/Whoever God is, I believe The Beloved is pure love, light and life. Nothing/nobody loves us more and nobody or nothing is more concerned about our happiness and well-being. God is permanent. I do believe our loved ones who have died are with God and that we will be re-united with them when we die. I believe that life after death is a certainty.

Too many negative labels have been attached to God. Throughout the ages, people have fought over whose god is the right and only god and slaughtered and plundered in order to prove it. We have slaughtered in the name of God! We have gone on crusades to spread the news of LOVE and either converted or killed in His name! It is utterly preposterous to think that the Almighty needs us to protect His honor! Strife, betrayal, plunder, rape, murder – all in the name of God! Is it any wonder that people have turned against the Beloved? Man, with a few exceptions, has NOT done a good job at representing God.

Many shudder at the thought of the Beloved as Heavenly Father because they have shocking, painful images and memories of father figures. How can anyone have a healthy, positive concept of God as a caring, protective figure if he has a father with a cruel temper and who beats his mother, or/ and sexually assaults him or his mom?

Has the church and other world religious represented God in ways that inspire and encourage us to enquire and investigate for ourselves? We are all familiar with the many reports in the news about so-called representatives of God sexually and/or physically abusing children and then having their crimes hidden and ignored by the leadership of the church and thus, allowing the pedophiles freedom to continue their vile acts. In losing faith in churches and religion, we have lost faith in God. Our anger is directed at The Beloved. We feel betrayed by those we trusted as His representatives. We have abandoned God because we judged Him by the actions of human beings. This is a HUGE mistake. It is shameful and sad that the many who are doing The Beloved's work throughout the world, are being painted with the same tainted tar brush. News seldom highlights the deeds of the truly good people. This is a pity. News networks predominantly focus on the negative and sensational events in the world.

We have stopped listening to sermons or to anything faintly linked to churches and religion. We have stopped speaking to or expecting a reply from God. This is possibly a good thing. This can be the beginning of something new. Perhaps we have listened for too long and too much to the opinions of others concerning the Beloved - especially those who claim to represent Him. Are we content to listen to the priest etc. expound on and explain God and scripture to us? We seldom question the interpretations and neither are we encouraged to delve into the sacred writings ourselves. We are spiritually lazy. It is easier to sit in a pew and let someone else do the delving and interpreting.

God is used as the ultimate weapon. He always has been and will always be so-used. What else carries as much fervent emotion as the idea of God fighting for you and your country? Religion and politics, when combined, make a powerful weapon. Look around you! Can you detect how and where they are is being co-used? Wars have been and are being carried out in The Almighty's name! The mention of "God" stirs up deep and powerful emotions i.e. fear, guilt, hatred, anger - to name but a few. These powerful emotions are purposefully used for political and religious ends. It is absolutely sinful and abhorrent the way God has been; is used and abused! The only way we can discover God, is to find out for ourselves.

This requires willingness and an inner journey will be required. Expect to be surprised!

Coo'ee My dearest,

Can you hear me? Are you listening? I have never stopped listening to you. I hear EVERY thought, word and sigh you think and express. The world is full of strident, loud noise. I will not compete with noise. I coo to you. I speak in soft, gentle murmurings of love. In order to hear me, you have to withdraw from noise. I do not and will not shout.

I watch people attempting to escape from the world through the distraction of noise. Some people have ear-plugs in their ears and pipe music directly into their ear canals hourly and daily! Who hears the gentle, soft sounds of rain, a sigh of the wind, a bird singing?

My dear one, I whisper in a soft voice. I have no need or desire to shout. My voice is within you. I AM within you. I AM the center of you. I AM signaling to you. Can you hear me?

CHAPTER TWO

TIDAL WAVES OF INFORMATION

We are satiated and bloated with information. We ingest too much of it. Tsunamis of information smash into us daily. Too many people and organization are bombarding us with relentless, useless, information. We might be informed but we are suffocating beneath the information weight.

Information is not wisdom. Information informs. It is a method of gaining knowledge. Too much junk information results in junk knowledge. Information does not always result in insight and understanding. To understand requires applied mental effort. A person understands when he grasps and comprehends the meaning of, the significance of, the nature and the explanation of. Thus, it is glaring obvious that much of the information we receive is directed at the five senses. Oh yes, we are certainly informed about many, many things and matters! No one refutes this -however understanding, worthwhile knowledge and wisdom are not the by-products of the senses.

Wisdom requires a personal quest. It demands effort. It isn't cheap neither easy to obtain. Wisdom won't come in pamphlet form. A person has to want it and seek it. One must undertake an inward journey. Wisdom can't be bought and nobody else can acquire it for us. It demands searching and sifting. A person has to hone the ability to sift - truth from falsity, right from wrong, good from evil and what is healthy from unhealthy. It results in the ability to make good judgements. A person can only embrace wisdom. It is a reward for personal knowledge that has been attained through effort, study, insight and experience.

21st century man is lazy and flabby. Mankind demands instant gratification. Information only requires the press of a single button.

Businesses know that modern man is lazy and demands to be spoon-fed. They comply and inform him what he needs, why he needs it, when he needs it and why the product will make him special, happy and important. Their services and products appear easy to obtain and effortless to pay for. Plastic money is money! Popping a credit or debit card into a handy counter machine isn't as painful as counting out hard-earned cash! Advertisements create desire for instant gratification. Is it any wonder that mankind is enslaved and manacled by the invisible chains of debt?

Governments also are to blame for the lack of wisdom in societies. Politicians make extravagant promises before elections that appeal - not to the necessities of people but to their wants. Some governments act like doting mammies who spoil their children, making them weak and dependent instead of strong, self-reliant and independent. Politicians know that if they don't molly-coddle voters they will be kicked out of office and replaced by a politician who will. Some politicians act like spoilt children themselves and abuse power by squandering the country's national purse in reckless investments and through indulging in self-enrichment!

The world is frantically searching for someone to solve the many issues and crises that are gripping it. Herein is GREAT danger. An informed, knowledgeable person is not necessary a wise person. History has shown this time-and-time again. Why aren't we seeking wise people to lead us? Why aren't we endeavoring to become wise ourselves?

Consider the many types of information: advertising, pamphlets, radio, newspapers, television, computers............ Aren't you fed-up with being accosted by the pleading/begging advertisements on television? The most emotionally-charged images are used to illicit maximum emotional response. It is emotionally draining and guilt entrapment! I am left with the overriding feeling that the world is a pit of endless suffering and sorrow. The truth though is that many governments, world-wide, waste vast amounts of money on ill-considered projects, corruption, nepotism, inefficiency and theft! Leaders from too many countries rely on the sympathy of the rest of the world to fix their humanitarian problems when they have the capacity and means to do so without resorting to international aid. Whenever I see images of war-torn, poor countries, I see belt upon belt of bullets strung across shoulders of soldiers, huge guns, trucks, machine guns and tanks! If they can afford to buy arms and armaments, then surely, they can feed their people! Houses, offices and shops are in ruins and reduced to rubble! It doesn't take any intelligence or effort to murder, rape and destroy. The same can be said about reducing a temple or shrine that has survived for thousands of years to piles of rocks and powder.

The incessant noise of populations complaining, waffling of politicians, relentless "Please Give….." appeals, uninspiring and irrelevant sermons by jaded priests, ranting and ravings by religious fanatics, wailings for calls to prayers, constant din of planes, revving cars, blaring radios, screaming television sets are tidal waves of mass din. Confused and anxiety-riddled populations are the result. People are buckling under the insane load of sensory bombardment. Who do we listen to? Whom can we trust? Who will listen to us? Who takes notice?

Businesses bombard us with information because they know we are too exhausted to go through masses of fine print. We sign on the dotted line or we renew our membership or subscription simply because we don't have the energy or time to study the documents and information. This is criminal coercion!

I often see a notice on my computer that requests me to enable or disenable something. It transpires that when I enable something on my laptop, it results in a slower computer. I want a fast computer so I obey and disenable. We are becoming disenabled! We sense a slowing down within and are vaguely aware that something is slowing us but we don't know the cause so we limp along.

This is the age of the "professional". We become disenabled by the belief that we can't do simple things and jobs ourselves and that we require a professional. Professional services are pricey! Naturally, there will be times when we will need to seek out a professional i.e. a dentist, a doctor, but, let's face it – we have been conned into believing we need others to do things that we are capable of doing ourselves! Somethings may require training but there are many, many things we can learn to do ourselves instead of instinctively turning to a professional. Self-reliance is readily surrendered and we are becoming too reliant on others. The world, with its ever-expanding population, requires employment – thus, professions are popping up everywhere. God forbid that we cut our own child's hair, bake our own scones or that your husband should paint the house! Do we really need a dietician to inform us that too much sugar is bad for us or consult a body-trainer to tell us that we need to exercise more? We can't even walk anymore without donning the most technologically advanced walking shoes! My white-washed takes (canvas-covered, white sport shoes) did just fine when I was young! We believe we have to wear designer clothes with upmarket prices and elite labels if we are to look fashionable. Labels define us! The price-tag on some items of clothing leaves us speechless – slavishly, we buy them anyway.

We are led to believe we need a priest/pastor/rabbi/guru/shaman/emir (spiritual professionals!) to tell us how to pray, what to pray, how long to pray, where to pray, where not to pray, where to worship, where not to worship, who is going to heaven, who is going to hell, how to get to heaven, whose god is the only god, which path is the true and only path, how many Hail Mary's to say – ad infinitum. Do we need a spiritual director/professional to find God or have a God-experience? We are spiritually disenabled and maimed if we believe we need a pope, priest, pastor, guru, shaman or some "spiritually advanced" person to enable us to encounter God! We must apply and exert ourselves if want to become spiritually wise. Spiritual wisdom demands exertion! Sitting in a pew or going through rituals does not, automatically, confer spiritual insight, understanding or wisdom. Words or/and deeds without sincerity are paper-thin - there is no depth! There isn't an effortless and instantaneous road to enlightenment and wisdom.

Part of the allure of hiring a professional is the belief that we don't have the time. It is less time-consuming to simply consult and pay. But, is this healthy and right? Most of us lead busy lives, it is true, but the last time I checked there are still 60 seconds to a minute, 60 minutes to the hour and 24 hours in a day! Just how did our grandparents and parents manage to do what they did without our modern, time-saving appliances and fast cars?

Thank goodness nature has refused to comply and adapt to our mad pace of life and mode of living! Autumn slowly approaches and the leaves lose their grip. Trees fall asleep in winter. Spring arrives and the buds and blossoms open. Summer bursts on the scene with its fruits and long days. Nature is truly wise. How unwise of us to get out of rhythm with it! We are paying a terrible price for so doing. Wisdom walks in step with nature. Birds return to their nests at sunset and stretch out their wings at sunrise because they are attuned to nature. We are not. We are out of harmony with it and our health is in decline as a result. Young children are glued to the computer or television way past their bed time and wake up grumpy and tired the next morning.

Many people are spiritually confused and lost. Some kill with the claim they do so because those they murder are unbelievers! Spiritual madness seems to be everywhere. We are rudderless and the ship is heading straight for the rocks. We are shipwrecking our souls. To whom must we turn? Where do we go for wise guidance?

Secondary post-traumatic stress is being experienced by much of the world's population due to the senses and mind continually being assaulted by sounds and images that induce fear, stress and trauma. The modern world is traumatic and disease-inducing! Is it any wonder that hospitals and health care services, even in first-world countries, are collapsing because they can no longer cope with the ever-increasing number of people requiring health care and hospitalization? Some claim it is due to people living longer but the "sickening" truth is that the sick range in age from the very young to the very old. Even eleven year-old children are suffering from diabetes! Something is very wrong with modern man!

Coo'ee, God is calling. He won't send us pamphlets, entertain or shout from a radio. There is loads of information about God and a great deal of it has been altered and perverted. If you have ears, listen! Can you hear the Beloved? He is cooing to you in love and gentleness. Put aside the information tsunami. The Almighty refuses to compete with noise and haste. Search for God and find wisdom – true wisdom.

God isn't cheap. We can't buy God! He isn't a figure on a gold chain around a neck. I AM! Put away the laptop, books - switch-off the radio, iPod, iPad, television etc. and search for Him. If you search for God, you will find God. Make time for the Beloved. We have time for everything else. It isn't difficult to find the Creator for He is everywhere. We don't have to go to church, ascend a mountain, sit in a temple or attend a mosque to find Him. No building can contain God and neither can any book - no matter how thick or revered. A book can't fully explain God. He cannot be confined between walls or the covers of books! Sit under a tree and listen to the Beloved coo through the sighing of the wind. Look into a baby's eyes and heart-listen to the song of a bird.

You are unique! God created you. The Beloved is never too busy for you for you are precious to Him. He cares for you more than you can imagine! You don't need words to talk to Him for He listens to your heart. He knows when you laugh and when you cry. You are an open-book to the Creator.

Coo'ee My dear one,

I AM not far from you. I AM within you. Never will I forsake you; never will I leave you.

You will never just be a face in a crowd or a mere number to Me. You are My beloved, unique child.

In a world, where all your attention is drawn outward, turn inward. Find Me. I am the True, Living Treasure. I AM the Pearl of great price.

Softly, gently I am calling your name. Come home to Me!

CHAPTER THREE

A GLUT OF GADGETS

I saw a program on television about hoarders in America and the distress it causes them and their loved ones. The occupant of the house has so much "stuff" that he can't navigate a path from one end of a room to the other end! Every room, crevice and nookie is crammed full of things he imagines he can't live without. Some of the goods are perishable and rotting! Such large-scale hoarding is a health and fire hazard!

What causes hoarding? Is it the belief that the more stuff we have, the happier we will be? Does this type of compulsive behavior make one feel more secure? Does it stem from fear of lack? Compulsive, obsessive hoarding is a complex problem.

We are living in a lopsided world regarding income and goods. Some poor countries with very large populations are constantly in need of basic necessities whilst affluent countries have surpluses of merchandise and food. Certain countries mass-produce cheap products and merchandise and sell it mostly to western countries that seem to have an insatiable appetite for it. Such is our topsy-turvy world!

As unthinkable as it is, countries have dumped millions of liters of milk because of a surplus and to keep the price "competitive"! The same applies to butter, fruit and other perishable, valuable foods. This, at a time when we are told that thousands of people die daily from starvation! I am sure there are plausible explanations that make "economic" sense for the dumping of food.e. logistics and cost of transportation of perishable food to areas where they are needed. However, wanton dumping of food still seem like madness to me.

We are urged to buy the latest gadget. The pace is relentless. The latest, "must-have" gadget is obsolete as soon as tomorrow. Yesterday's mobile phone is a brick compared to today's latest slim, micro-chipped packed wafer-thin mobile. The same rapid turn-over pace applies to computers, watches, and DVD players – almost everything!

The target market, obviously, is not the elderly. It's not uncommon to see a middle-aged person battling to press minute buttons on a smartphone or poised, uncertainly, with a stylus over a smartphone menu panel. Just when a senior citizen gets used to operating the ATM; it is upgraded into something more complicated, quicker, smarter and option-overloaded!

Look at our garbage disposal sites! They are ever-growing mountains of garbage and discarded gadgets. I'm told that many of the components in our electronic appliances are hazardous and should never be disposed of at a site. Nature knows nothing of tins, boxes and plastic. Nature's packaging is disposable and biodegradable i.e. a banana skin, a coconut shell, a berry skin, and so forth. Most manmade packaging is non-biodegradable and causes untold suffering and death when it finds its way into rivers, lakes and oceans. Man's garbage is disposed of every day - multiply that by 365 days and you get an idea how much toxic waste we dispose of every year! Ever increasingly, our once beautiful planet is becoming a stinking, rotting dumping site of toxic waste emitting poisonous gases!

Much of what is manufactured today is sub-standard quality because good quality lasts longer. There is more money to be made in quantity. Why repair something when it is cheaper to replace it? Why mend socks when we can buy a pack of six pairs for less than the price of cotton and a needle? How much more can our long- suffering planet take before it revolts and says, "Enough"!

We are groomed and encouraged to want. We MUST have this or that product or that car. We no sooner have the "thing" than the ownership-glow wanes. We are obsessive-compulsive buyers. Shopping is fun until we get to the check-out and have to pay for the purchases. Some people feel hard-done by not being able to afford things - so they steal what they want. Haven't they been encouraged to own things? Aren't they entitled to own what their heart's desire? I saw a show on television where people "modelled" their stolen clothes and accessories and explained that they didn't see anything wrong in stealing because businesses have insurance so shoplifting can't be classified as theft! I have no idea what theft costs businesses annually, but, I am sure it runs into mega millions. Yet others make a living by taking orders from people then go steal the items and get a fee from the "customer"! Maybe some are driven through desperation due to high rates of unemployment, but, truth be told, most are too lazy to do an honest day's work.

How many things do we need to make us happy? How big should our house be before we feel content? How much should our car cost before we feel important? These are THINGS. Things are too important to us. Objects are more importance to us than God - that is idolatry!

We take better care of our cars than we do ourselves. Things are inanimate objects - they are senseless! People are not things. People have souls, tears, hearts, and feelings. Objects are incapable of love. They won't visit you when you are in hospital. They won't cry when you die and they are won't put flowers on your grave. Your mom will cry. Your dad will visit you in hospital. Your friends will remember you when you die. Someone will remember you and visit your grave. My brother, Bill, said: "I have never seen a truck unload a person's belongings at a funeral. Only people weep." How true! We have got it so VERY wrong! If an earthquake struck now, what would you save? What will be most precious to you?

I cannot end this chapter unless I also stress how this "gadget-mad" mentality has influenced our treatment of animals. Cruelty to animals is prevalent and frequent. Trophy hunting is popular today. People pay exorbitant amounts of money to "hunt" a wild animal with a high-powered, telescopic rifle. They pose for a photograph with their "kill" and some have the animal skinned and the skin shipped back to where they live as a trophy! The killing of rhinos for their horns and elephants for their tusks by well-organized, well-funded syndicates is sickening! Exotic birds, reptiles and rare animals are trapped and smuggled into countries by syndicates. It is disgusting, shocking and sickening. George and Joy Adamson weren't killed by the lions they tried to protect, but by humans! Dian Fossey was not killed by a silver-back gorilla but butchered by humans. Joy and George were elderly when they were slaughtered and Dian was alone and defenseless on a mountain when she too was slaughtered! Humans are the most dangerous predators on earth.

How can any right-minded person chain, beat, neglect or starve a pet? Puppy mills are inhumane places! The puppies and dogs are not regarded as creatures that feel pain, terror and fear but are treated with cold disdain. Last week, I read about a man in Canada who speared a large bear. The bear suffered, in agony, for hours before it was killed. The wannabe "hunter" posed atop the carcass of that magnificent creature, grinning like the eejit he obviously is. Recently, there was a photo of a young, glamorous woman holding a high-powered rifle posing next to her trophy - a giraffe! Give me a break! Jesus said not even one sparrow falls to the ground without God knowing about it!

God is not an object or a person. The Beloved is not a sweet-machine that pops out a treat whenever we pray! We think we appease God, force His forgiveness and squeeze the gift of eternal life out of Him if we push the right buttons. It isn't all that long ago that people paid for the forgiveness of sins!

While Moses was away receiving the Ten Commandments, the people became impatient and restless. They demanded the melting-down of gold to make a golden calf and worshipped the golden THING! No matter how many carats or ingots of gold went into the making of the golden calf; it was still just a lifeless, metallic golden calf! We too become restless and impatient. The danger is insidious and ominous. What are we worshipping today? Whatever God is - He isn't an inanimate, lifeless object! "I AM". God feels far deeper than any human being. The Beloved is not a gadget, an appliance, a metallic object, a golden calf or a manufactured thing. He is The Living I AM God.

Coo'ee My dear one,

How I long for you to know Me! I am the One who created you and who breathed life into you. Before you were born, I knew you. I have known you all your life.

I AM calling you. I care for and about you. I know you inside-out. You are precious to Me. Put aside your "things" and spend time with Me. In Me you find life - real life. Respect all living creatures. Things are inanimate and lifeless. Respect all life, especially those who can't defend themselves. I told Moses to take off his sandals because he was standing on holy ground. All ground is holy and must be trod on with reverence for I created it and it belongs to Me.

There is too much aggression and violence in the world. Be gentle.

Only the strong are strong enough to be gentle. The aggressive are weak and fear-full. Dare to be divinely human and feel with your heart and soul.

ECCLESIASTES 5:10-11

Whoever loves money
    never has money enough;
   whoever loves wealth
    is never satisfied
    with his income.
   This too is meaningless.
As goods increase,
   So do those who consume them.
And what benefits are they
    to the owner
   Except to feast his eyes on them?
(The Holy Bible: New International Version)

CHAPTER FOUR

UNHEARD, UNSEEN, APPRECIATED

Have you felt invisible? I have. The older I get, the more invisible I feel! Not only do I feel as if I am not seen but also not heard! Is it a figment of my imagination? Sadly, it isn't!

Suicide is a huge, distressing problem word-wide. Not many years ago, it was mostly middle-aged and elderly who committed suicide. Not so anymore! Today, young people are ending their lives - even children are killing themselves! Why is this? What is happening? Many families have, are, or will experience the tragedy of suicide. Parent's hearts and lives are ripped apart by the self-inflicted death of a son or daughter. Just what is so awful, terrible and unbearable that people are choosing to forfeit life through suicide? Doubtlessly, there are many reasons but for many it is because they have grown tired of been unheard, unseen and unappreciated. Not to be seen, heard or appreciated is terrible pain.

Life is distraction. We are constantly pulled in many directions. It's not that we DON'T want to hear, see or appreciate our beloved because we do, but life calls for our attention and demands response and action from us. We wear ourselves out trying to break-even at the close of day. The pace of modern life is relentless and soul-destroying. We promise ourselves that we will set aside time to focus on our loved ones and spend quality time with them, but, tomorrow arrives and the pattern repeats itself. The cycle will repeat itself unless we put a stop to it. STOP IT! Nothing is more important than your life and the well-being of your cherished ones. We aren't robots that have no option but to go, go, go. Tick-tock, the hands of the clock are moving! Let's not wake-up one morning with the sick realization that our parents have grown frail and old without us noticing or that our once small, cuddly children have flown the nest or that the person we married years ago is now a stranger!

I lost my youngest brother, Raymond, and my cousin, Eddy, to suicide. I know, firsthand, the desolation caused by suicide. I know all about guilt and the What-If's. I have experienced the deep chasm of failure and responsibility when my loved ones killed themselves. It's agonizing. I miss them every day - EVERY single day! I can't bring myself to peel back the emotions regarding this subject because it is so excruciatingly painful. Could I have prevented my brother's suicide if I had loved him more and listened to him more intently? I mean REALLY listened! Could I have prevented their lonely deaths if I had stopped to see them? I mean REALLY stopped to see them! Would they have felt that they mattered and were worthy if I had let them know how much I appreciate them? And I mean EXPRESSED appreciation. The truth is that hearing, seeing and acknowledging have become perfunctory, auto-pilot actions. We don't truly interact or experience the uniqueness of people. This has to stop if we are to avert the suicide of a loved one. NEVER assume that someone knows how much you love, respect and appreciate him or her.

SCHOOL PHOTO OF RAYMOND

Your eyes are big and bright,
full of wonder, full of light.
Your smile is happy and wide and
large ears protrude from your head on either side.
An innocent child aged six.

Both your cheeks have freckles galore and
your cute nose has even more.
Shoulders are straight and back
In your school blazer of white and black.

Your forehead is high and wide and
no lines of care run from middle to side.
A "light" is shining on your hair
as if an angel put it there.

A magnificent child aged six.
Now I look at another photo of you -
taken when you were thirty-two.
Gone is the smile and gone is the light.
Gone are the freckles and gone the sparkle of delight.
and the worn face no longer resembles the child I once knew.

Life can be cruel and unkind!
And can so easily bruise the soul and crush a heart and mind!
It eroded the innocence, glory, magnificence and joy
that once was you, a pristine, six-year old little boy.

We aren't dough cut with a cookie-cutter. People are similar and different. Each person is unique and each one has his/ her breaking point. Fishermen use different breaking strains when fishing. They know that some fish, such as marlin, are powerful and will require a strong line/ gut. A weak gut would snap. It will be silly to use a powerful gut to catch a sardine! Each type of fish is different and requires different breaking strains of gut. They are all fish but each one is different. The same applies to people. We are all people but each person is unique. Everyone has a different breaking point. What I can bear; another can't. What another bears, I may not be able to bear. It is ridiculous to expect someone else to cope because I can cope! Only God knows what each person can bear. Only The Beloved fully understands our heart, mind and soul.

I hasten to add that we cannot and must not crucify ourselves for the suicide of a loved one. We are human. We aren't angels and we are definitely not God. We are doing our best and loving as best we can. We can't read another's mind. Sometimes, people expect too much from us and we expect too much from ourselves. It is never easy to unburden yourself to another. Nobody wants to appear vulnerable, helpless or desperate. We wear a mask and it is difficult to unmask so that another can see the pain and distress. Jesus did. In the Garden of Gethsemane, He told His disciples that He was in anguish and distress. He asked them to stay with Him a while in His time of distress. Jesus never wore a mask. He didn't expect or ask them to take away His pain – all He wanted was companionship. The disciples fell asleep full knowing about His plight. Sometimes, we fall asleep whilst someone we know is in anguish! Jesus accurately described the human condition when He said that the spirit is willing but the flesh is weak. It's not that we don't care but that we are human.

Home ought to be the one place we are heard, seen, appreciated and where we feel that we belong and are wanted. When we leave the front door, we enter a world of strangers. Then we are the commuter, consumer, employee, a password, a number! We are stripped of our uniqueness and identity. With the exception of family and friends, we aren't anybody special or important. When I receive a notification or letter that has THE RESIDENT on the envelope, I bin it because I know whoever sent it doesn't know me or care about me.

Homes are under tremendous pressure. Can they be called home? The word "home" denotes a happy, safe environment and a family that loves and cherishes each other. That's my idea of home. For many, it isn't home but just a place where people live together. It can be a place filled with strife and tension, and, sometimes, unspeakable cruelty. Where do we go to be treated kindly, lovingly and with appreciation if we do not experience them at home or from our family?

Not long after Raymond committed suicide, I found myself in a bustling mall. He and I had often met there for coffee. The place was thronged with people. I scanned faces hopelessly wishing I would see his face again. In that instant, I experienced the irreplaceable uniqueness of Raymond. No face in that crowd was his nor could be his. How many times can a heart break? I know mine broke at that realization and it has broken many times since.

Are we heard in a world that is flooded with information and gadgets? REALLY listened to and heard? With so much visual bombardment - are we seen? One day I sat in my chair and focused all my attention on a friend. I brailed her with my eyes, absorbing all her facial features. She wasn't aware of what I was doing. In those few lingering minutes, I really SAW her. I experienced her. In the past, I had been like a butterfly in my interactions with people – lightly and briefly interacting. To experience something, one has to focus one's attention. It's akin to zooming-in. That is what it means to be seen, heard and appreciated.

The gone voice and phantom hands of a loved one breaks the heart and fills it to overflowing with unspeakable longing.

When someone is kind it is not because we are entitled to their kindness. There is too much talk of entitlement today. People don't have to be kind to us – but choose to be. There are many people in a person's life that he/she can choose to be kind to. You are gifted when someone selects you to focus on and express kindness to. Appreciate it.

Do people send Thank You cards and notes anymore? My heart still swells whenever I remember receiving a birthday bouquet of flowers from my uncle, Patrick. I hadn't expected it. I can still recall the thrill when a delivery man from a florist rang my doorbell and stood at my garden gate with the bouquet. A bouquet is more than flowers - it is a beautiful way of telling someone that they are remembered and celebrated. I felt special that day and the fact that I so clearly remember it is evidential to how deeply it touched me. Someone wrote a poem about giving flowers to a person whilst the person is alive rather than sending roses when s/he is dead and can't enjoy them. For some people, the only time they receive flowers, is at their funeral! Why, oh why, wait to bring flowers to a grave when you can give them to the person whilst alive? Do it today! Say it today! Every human being wants and yearns to know that s/he is loved, wanted and matters. We all want to know that our life had made a difference to someone.

Isolation is what we experience when we are not heard, seen or appreciated. Our lives are invisible. The elderly withdraw into their houses and long for the phone to ring or a letter to arrive. An elderly lady, who had lived alone for many years, was found dead in her apartment a few days after she died. Her diary was on her bedside cupboard. The same entry had been penned, day-after-day: "No one came today." There are children, teenagers and young people who also feel isolated and lonely. They mingle and laugh, but, deep within, they feel invisible.

Coo'ee My dear one,

Come to ME. You are the apple of My eye. My gaze is constantly upon you. I see you. I know you. You will never be reduced to a number by Me. Never! I call you by name. You are precious. Nothing is more important than you. I am never too busy for you.

I love your voice. I made it. I hear you. I hear your sighs, laughter and prayers. I know your mind and heart. I don't need words to hear or understand you.

My dear one, I want to thank you! You have brought joy to people and you have made my world more wonderful and beautiful because of you. You are brave and courageous! To face life and the world with such courage is astounding! Thank you for helping someone, for being kind and for walking beside one who is slower or weaker than you.

Often remind yourself that you are never alone. Nobody lives alone and no one will ever die alone. I walk with you. There are forces and beings that you cannot see. They are with you on your life journey and they cheer you on. No matter what happens; know I love you and that I will NEVER, NEVER forsake you nor EVER, EVER leave you. Keep on keeping on. I AM with you.

CHAPTER FIVE

NOISE IS POISON

Nature isn't noise-packed. Thunder is loud but not jarring. The sounds of nature are mostly melodious and soothing. The sigh of a soft breeze, the pitter-patter of rain, a gurgling brook and giggling waves are medicine to the soul. Today, I listened to a bird singing in a nearby tree. Enchanting!

We are estranged and divorced from nature. It is mauled and savaged as populations grow and the demand for houses, apartments and shopping malls increases. Forests are shrinking as trees are felled for quick profit and the ground claimed for cattle farming. Birds and animals are left homeless. Where do animals and birds go when their habitation is destroyed? The songs of birds singing and animals calling to each other are smothered by whining chainsaws. Clean air is replaced by diesel and other toxic fumes. Rivers are diverted, dammed and polluted. Fracking pumps toxic chemicals into the ground and aquafers. The music of nature is being silenced.

I was watching a tennis match being played at Wimbledon. At a point during the match, there was noise in the audience. The umpire pulled the microphone towards her and said, "Quiet. Silence please!" A hush followed. Sometimes I wish I could command silence! I was with a friend in a coffee shop recently but it was spoilt by loud, jarring "music" blaring through speakers. To make matters worse, a busker pulled out his guitar, connected it to an amplifier, and started to play it outside the shop! If one wants hush or silence; a town, city or where-ever man is, is not the place one will find them. Modern man can't cope with silence or with being still. Why is silence frightening? Could it be that when we enter silence and stillness, we encounter ourselves? Noise and constant motion are buffers against awareness of our mortality and fragility. Not all sound is noise. Some sounds are marvelous, uplifting and healthy. The sound of children laughing is soul-music. A bird trilling in a tree, the rustling of leaves in autumn and the murmuring of slow-flowing water calms and replenishes both mind and nervous system.

The majority of modern sounds are manmade and the music of nature is receding rapidly. The thud of jack hammers, shrill hedge trimmers, whirring lawnmowers, shrieking strimmers (weed-eaters) etc. can't compete with the sounds of nature! Just one of these mechanical noises is detrimental to our nervous system but in addition there are: the drone of planes, whining motor cars, screaming sirens, pulsating and (sometimes) nauseating "music", honking hooters etc. This is insanity! Our ears and nerves are continually being assaulted and damaged by manmade noise.

Years ago, when Iraq invaded Kuwait I read an article in a newspaper that still saddens me. The animals in the zoo in Kuwait were traumatized by the sounds of shooting and bombs exploding. Many of them starved to death but some survived. One them was an adult elephant. It was exhausted and terrified. After the Iraqi forces withdrew, the zoo was renovated. The renovations were accompanied by the noise of machines. The traumatized elephant killed itself by pounding its head against a wall! The added noise of rebuilding was more than it could bear.

Many people feel the wrap-around noise of modern life is pushing them to the wall. With already exhausted nervous systems, the addition of one more synapse-destroying sound can cause complete collapse. Depression is the result of nervous system overload and depletion. In my gran's days it was called a nervous breakdown. The brain absorbs what the senses feed it and repetitive, monotonous noise causes nervous exhaustion. Our bodies are miracles but they can only bear so much before the weight of sensory overload causes them to collapse. Much has been written about sensory deprivation as a form of torture during wars but today populations are being tortured by sensory overload! This is especially true concerning the auditory bombardment of noise. Excessive, continual exposure to noise IS hazardous.

What's the solution? How wonderful if we could simply ban the use of certain machines, however, this is unlikely. It is more probable that noise will increase. Our machines are getting bigger and noisier. We dig deeper, cut through more mountains and send more satellites and rockets into space. Progress comes at a price and we and our planet are paying the price. All of life on earth is paying the price. Unless something, on a global scale, happens soon that will force mankind to take less and allow nature to recuperate; I don't see light at the end of the tunnel!

I was in the ICU ward when my brother, Bill, was very ill. I was astonished to see a man talking on a mobile phone, despite signage that requested that all mobile phones be switched off! The sign clearly stated that the use of mobile phones could affect the specialized equipment used in ICU. Not one staff member intervened! The man's selfish disregard defied comprehension.

Being ill and in hospital is a stressful experience. Patients need a relaxed, quiet, calm surrounding. Doctors of yore knew that the environment must be conducive to healing for optimal patient recovery. Green walls assisted in the healing process due to its calming effect. Windows were opened to allow in fresh air. Not so today! Now hospitals are noisy places. Walls are painted a glaring white. Air-conditioned (recycled) air is circulated to keep temperatures constant. How healthy can it be for stale air to circulate in an environment that is already jam-packed with germs?

Hospitals are now businesses. Targets must be met. There is an ever-increasing demand for hospitals as populations soar and resources dwindle. The fortunate can afford private hospitals and top-notch medical aids, and, consequential peace of mind but those who are reliant on state hospitals put their lives at risk.

Some of the poorer countries have few or no hospitals and are in dire need of medically trained and qualified nurses and doctors. Some of the hospitals are unhygienic and not conducive to recuperation. Recovery in these places is nothing short of a miracle. Western countries lure medically trained professionals from these poorer countries with attractive salaries and benefits, thus leaving them medically impoverished!

It is a sad state of affairs that hospitals are becoming luxuries! Why are people becoming sicker and not healthier? Why is medical treatment so expensive and why are hospitals so costly? Our forefathers lived in a world that wasn't as polluted, toxic or as technically advanced as the world is today, yet, it seems they were healthier than we are! Diabetes is now common in children! It's not surprising when one considers the amount of sugar that is consumed and our inactive, modern lifestyles. Our planet is so degraded that it is becoming increasingly difficult to stay healthy.

Who can solve the noise problem? All of us will have to take responsibility for personal noise management. We can meditate. We quieten the mind in order to contemplate something – be it a rose, photo, poem or a picture. It is also an opportunity for God to talk to us. When we pray, we talk to Him but when we quieten the mind, God talks to us. The Beloved does not compete with noise. We have grown God-deaf so it may take time before we hear His cooing. Relax, be still and quiet and let its soothing effects calm the jangled, frazzled nerves and frantic mind.

Even places of worship are noisy! Gone are the days when chatter ended at the front door of the Church. Churches were holy, hushed places of reverence - now people chatter inside. It is an open display of disrespect for God and a lack of consideration for fellow-worshippers. The world is a noisy place but we do we have to bring the world inside houses of worship and prayer?

Music can be balm to the soul. Vibrations and frequencies either deplete or uplift. Marinade yourself in "good" music. Take a picnic away from city noise. Laugh more. Incessant chatter drains both chatterer and listener. Language should be soothing, uplifting and healing. Modern language is strident, crude and aggressive. Some words are musical and paint wonderful mental pictures but foul language is foul. It pollutes. It strains the mind and nervous system. I hear people using the most disgusting and aggressive words in everyday, public conversations! Recently, a friend of mine remarked that she was aghast at the use of filthy language used in a television program. It was supposed to be a "family program" and she hadn't expected to be confronted by gutter language. She stated, "It felt that violence was being inflicted on me!" She was right – vulgar, foul language is violent and a form of violence.

It is incorrect to say that only sticks and stones can break bones – words break hearts. Words are powerful. Beautiful, young people have committed suicide due to cruel words said to them. Words can be as lethal as poison. Conversely, they can be used to instill hope, encouragement and cheer. Use your words wisely. People are imprisoned for murder yet many people are verbally murdered yet the perpetrator is seldom held accountable. To destroy life through the use of physical or verbal assault is murder.

MAMMA EARTH

My darling mamma earth
what have we done to you?
Dirty rivers, dirty seas, dirty sky
Oh Lord, my soul wants to cry, cry, cry
for my darling earth mother
who through greed, is made to suffer!
Our darling mother earth
what have we done to you?
Tar, concrete, bricks and cities of steel
Oh Lord, Oh God, please heal, heal, and heal
our beloved earth mother
who, because of us, is made to suffer!

Your darling mother earth –
what are you doing to her?
Wounded, tortured, raped - you make her bleed
for quick profit and insatiable greed.
Oh, please don't forget, don't neglect earth mother
Please, oh please, don't let her suffer.

Oh mother earth
you are our matriarch,
our hope and our rock.
Forgive us our trespasses
and guard the hills and all grasses.
Restore, restore, oh, - please restore
we genuflect, we beseech, we humbly implore.

Coo'ee My dear one,

Are you tired? Are you weary? Is your heart heavy-laden? Come to Me.
In Me you will find an oasis in the desert of life. The world parches you
with its harshness. I am Living Water. I WILL refresh and revive your
flagging spirit.

Carefully choose the words you want to seep into your inner being.

You can't always choose what you hear but you can choose the words you want to take root in your heart and mind. Listen to My words. My Words are life-giving. Believe them. I AM not a mirage that promises much but produces nothing.

Withdraw from the world for your own sake. Take a holiday from the world. The green I made in nature is healing. Spend time in the living green. Spend time where you can listen to and hear the sounds of nature.

Beloved of Mine, Be Still and Know that I AM ....God. You need not fear Me. Why should you fear Me? There is much to be afraid of in life but I AM with you. Find refuge and strength in Me when people and life threaten to overwhelm you.

I AM waiting for you. Don't be afraid and troubled. I AM a Pool Of Peace and Serenity.

CHAPTER SIX

PHONY AND LONELY

Recently, I saw a beautiful flower. It was in a vase in a restaurant. The colors were magnificent. I put out my hand to touch its green, slender stem only to discover it was a fake. It was an artificial! We can make flowers, trees and shrubs so life-like that it is almost impossible to distinguish between what is alive and what is plastic. We can purchase fake, lifelike grass too. Artificial plants and vegetation don't require the bother of being watered or fertilized and they maintain their fake "floral beauty" throughout the year. They are low-maintenance and relatively inexpensive - price being determined by the quality of fakeness. Why toil and care for living plants? The major difference between the two is that artificial plants are lifeless, sterile and give zilch whilst "real" plants are alive, fertile and are generous.

It's difficult to distinguish a genuine from a phony person. Don't trust everyone who whispers, "Trust me". Some people make promises they know are untrue and have no intention of honoring. Whom can we trust? Whom should we trust? Jesus said: "You will know a tree by its fruit". Words are cheap. They are as copious as leaves on a summer tree. Actions are fruit. True friends express themselves through action. They give. They walk with you through thick and thin whilst false friends either don't turn up or desert you when you need them. Countless people have lost their hard-earned money by putting their trust in a fake person and yet others have lost more than money by not being able to distinguish between a counterfeit and genuine person.

Doping and cheating are rampant in sport. Some "athletes" have won races, medals, fame and fortune knowing, full-well, that they cheated by using steroids and other banned drugs. What sense of accomplishment can be had by cheating in order to win? The only incentive for cheating; is money. Fake/phony athletes! Too many genuine sportsmen/women have been cheated in sport and reaping the hard-earned rewards. When a cheater is exposed for doping, you would expect to see him/her shame-faced, but, to the contrary, they appear arrogant. Sadly, it is difficult to identify the cheat from the disciplined, honest, decent athlete.

Mankind forgets that there is no such thing as a secret. Cain forgot this when he murdered his brother, Abel. There is always a Witness. When Moses killed an Egyptian and buried him in the desert, thinking no one saw his deed, he too was mistaken. We can fool others, we can fool ourselves, but, we can't fool God! The Beloved is omnipresent, omniscient and omnipotent.

There was a charity that was established to support families traumatized by the suicide of a loved one. Millions of Euros were collected. The news broke recently about the "alleged" misuse of large amounts of money by the CEO. Overseas holidays, purchases of groceries, clothing and suchlike for personal use and for his family were bought and paid for by using credit cards that belong to the charity! Money was diverted and squandered on the CEO and his family! The extent of the fraud is still under investigation. The CEO was a phony philanthropist - a fake Good Samaritan! How can we recognize a genuine philanthropist? How can we distinguish a real Good Samaritan from a Bad Samaritan? By their fruit (deeds/actions) they reveal who and what they are.

Due to tampering with nature, we have produced de-scented flowers! Surely, this is a crime against nature? They may be robust and resistant to disease and bugs, but, who wants a de-perfumed flower? Their essential uniqueness has been sabotaged! What is a rose without its scent? What is a garden without heady perfume? Can you imagine lavender not smelling like lavender? We may have produced plants that are sturdier than their scented relatives but the price is too high. We need the scents of nature more than ever as our planet stinks more and more from manmade toxins, gasses and fumes. What about bee populations that are declining alarmingly world-wide due to the intolerable over-use of chemicals, global warming and the greenhouse effect? We must protect these amazing creatures and assist them by providing them with perfumed flowers and plants.

Who or what is draining perfume from your inner being? Each person is unique and has a unique vibration. Vast amounts of money are spent on the production of chemical perfumes. Some film stars have their own perfume brand. Phony scents are everywhere - shower gels, soaps, underarm deodorants, aftershave foams, car deodorizers, shoe deodorizers etc. We can install a device in our home that pumps out chemical aromatic scents at timed intervals. You can buy sea, meadow, or citrus scented candles! The variety and spectrum of phony scents is mind-boggling. We mask hazardous household chemicals with names such as: Lemon Fresh, Pine Forest, Meadow Fresh, Eden Orchard and Marine Heaven. Meadow Delight, Sea Burst or Citrus Delight is used to odorize our laundry. We mimic the fragrances of nature because nature is receding so rapidly. There is no substitute for the smell of a baby, the milky burp of a puppy, the cologne on granny's handkerchief, the heady smell of mom's cake baking in the oven and the powdery smell of new rain on dry, caked soil! They are God created perfumes that remind us that our planet is a living garden.

We leave a part of ourselves whenever and wherever we interact and it either enriches or impoverishes. We are also enriched or impoverished by others. We sense the impact of the interaction via vibration. Vibrations can't be manipulated or masked. What a person truly is; is felt as vibration. It is the essence of who and what we are. How do person make you feel when you are with them? Do you feel - uplifted, encouraged, invigorated, enlivened, joyful, light, or: depleted, jagged, deflated and belittled? What impact do we make on others? Jesus said it is impossible to obtain pure water from a fountain filled with dirty water. What's inside will reveal itself. Let' fill up our lives with the fragrances of gentleness, kindness, patience and love. The world is sick of the stench of fakeness and is longing for the genuine aroma of goodness. Crime, bribery, nepotism, cruelty, violence, corruption, greed and their like are stenches that nauseate mankind to the core. God gave us a garden and entrusted it to our care fully expecting us to act as custodian gardener. We are to be its protector - not its polluter!

Grains are being genetically modified. I believe it is with the intention of making them grow quicker and to become insect resistant. As the world's population keeps expanding; so the demand for food increases. Food security is vital for national and international security. I don't know the consequences of genetically tinkering with grains and seeds; however, I do know that there is great concern and disquiet regarding the unforeseen repercussions of such genetic modification.

Not only are grains being genetically modified, but so too are human beings! Doubtlessly, wonderful medical discoveries await us in the field of genetic manipulation. The problem is that man doesn't know when to stop tinkering! Not content with old-fashion bombs; man created atomic and hydrogen bombs! God only knows what man is busy developing today - the imagination boggles. Then there are the medical experiments in cosmetic plastic surgery. Modern man worships youth and wants to resist the aging process by turning to cosmetic plastic surgery. There is a concerted effort, especially in the West, to delay and defy ageing along with its concomitant wrinkles and sagging. Women spend fortunes on wrinkle-delaying potions and lotions and now men are following suite. Some eternal youth seekers have emerged from cosmetic plastic surgery looking more feline than human! There is only so much surgery can do! I emerged from coloring my hair auburn recently only to nearly faint when I saw my reflection in a mirror – I looked like an orangutan! Ah vanity – all is vanity!

I was listening to the radio. An author was being interviewed and her subject was startling and alarming. When the Cold War came to an end, America was horrified to find that it was lagging far behind the former Soviet Union regarding biological experiments. Russia, it transpires, had a number of biologists working for it in the development of biologically advanced soldiers. The Pentagon, at this stage, did not have even one biologist on its staff. This was soon remedied. Developments are well underway to produce a substance that will render soldiers devoid of pain when injured in battle! The most alarming part of her research is the fact that scientists and biologists are developing the amalgamation (amalgamated) human! I think that's the word she used. Microchips will be implanted into the brain that will enhance hearing to extraordinary levels and eyes will be able to see in the dark and see colors not normally detected. Microchips inserted into the human brain will determine and govern actions and behavior! Experiments have already been carried out on mice. I heard an excited scientist tell how by placing electrodes into the brain of a mouse and applying electrical charges, it can cause it to react fearfully at seeing something as neutral and as harmless as a paper clip. Modified behavior!

Mankind is on its way to producing the merging of human and robot- it is referred to as "amalgamation". Artificial intelligence is being developed. God only knows when we will cross the line of no return – if we haven't already! It reminds me of the story of Frankenstein! Huge and wonderful medical advances can be made regarding microchips - for example: restoring movement to paralyzed limbs, sight to blind eyes and hearing to deaf ears. The question is whether mankind will use this knowledge to kill or heal; to save or destroy. We need to remind ourselves that in the 2nd World War concentration camps it was intelligent, medically trained people who experimented in the most horrendous and horrifying ways on helpless people they regarded as sub-human beings.

A few days ago, I heard a representative of Microsoft saying that she had a number of meetings with Bill Gates and corporate members of Microsoft to discuss future use of robots and artificial intelligence and how it will impact of humans and life as we know it. This lady went on to state that for every one use of artificial intelligence; ten men and twenty women would be made redundant. Hello! Am I missing something here? Won't artificial intelligence, bots, robots and "amalgams" result in massive unemployment? I know I'm human but I do know that the use of AI and robots as replacements for human labor will result in people becoming redundant – as labor and as people! Are these so-called advances an attempt to by-pass humans and, consequentially, solve the problem of trade unions, strikes, pay increase demands, low productivity levels, laziness and abuse of the labor laws? What will the masses of unemployed do every day - watch boxsets of television programs? Where will governments get the taxes to provide for the many services i.e. hospital, schools etc.? How will governments pay the idle masses?

Why are the Chief Executive Officers, executives and members of boards, paid such massive salaries plus bonuses? A robot won't pay taxes. But, and, this is an alarming thought – could it be that the intention behind AI and advances in robots is the domination of mankind? Mankind will be rendered servile and obedient and "policed" by artificial intelligent, "amalgamations" and robots! I remember how I guffawed when a manufacturer of computers stated that the advent of computers would result in a paperless society. Chortle, chortle, chortle!

Cyber-attacks are on the increase. We hear, daily, that secure and protected data has been hacked. It is reported that the latest USA presidential election was hacked! On Sunday I went to a supermarket and was met by a large sign in the windows that stated: "Cash payment only. Computers are off-line" Oh, for the days of paper and pen.

The oldest game is the blame game. Adam blamed Eve for eating the forbidden fruit - actually, he blamed God: "The woman You gave" etc. Eve blamed Adam. The unwillingness to assume personal responsibility preceded blaming. The game continues today. The tragedy is when we play the game so often, so successfully, we no longer know that we are playing it. It controls us and we become the game. Values and morals become blurred. We no longer know right from wrong, honest from dishonest, truth from lies, good from evil. We have lost our inner compass. The three witches in Shakespeare's Macbeth said: "Fair is foul and foul is fair." What was considered fair yesterday is regarded as foul today and vice versa. Murder is sanctified when someone deems it fit to do so, done in God's name, or as revenge. We can justify and blame as much as we like, but whether we like it or not, we will have to take responsibility before God and account for our choices, decisions and actions.

At breakfast, my eyes came to rest on a tub of margarine on the table. On it was emblazoned the words, "Just like Butter", then in smaller type, "A rich, buttery spread." It may look like butter, it may taste like butter – but, it isn't butter. Butter is butter. The Afrikaans people have a wonderful and accurate name for margarine – Kunsbotter (artificial butter). Margarine is artificial butter. So much food is artificial food. They look like ………. but, they aren't. There is a saying: "If it quacks like a duck, walks like a duck; then it is a duck." Manufacturers make their products to sound and taste like the original, natural product but they are phonies. The same truth applies to people - they may sound, look and act like genuine people but they are phonies. They are fakes. A person may be friendly but that doesn't mean he/she is a friend. An honest person is honest. A friend is a friend. It's as simple as that. A genuine person's values, principles and morals are not at odds with his/her behavior. A phony, counterfeit, imitation, veneer person can't be consistent in words, actions and behavior. A liar needs a long and good memory if s/he isn't to be exposed as a fraud. Who wants to live like that? Who wants to be a fake?

It is disheartening but this is the world we live in. It's not surprising that people are suffering from acute anxiety and loneliness. Being with people does not immunize us against loneliness. We can be, and sometimes are, at our loneliest in the center of a crowd. Some people even feel lonely in their own family! Sometimes, we feel lonely at our place of work and with our co-workers. Many children feel isolated in school. Despite the risks, we must continue to reach out. There will always be the bully, gossiper, back-stabber, deserter, traitor but there will also be the loyal, true, kind, gentle, faithful, loyal, honest, and brave too. These are worth searching for. We aren't timid, fragile snails who withdraw into shells whenever our outreaches are met with rebuff. We must avoid withdrawing into shells. Of course, we may get disappointed, hurt and discouraged but let's stick our necks out until we find people worth finding.

Coo'ee My dear one,

I AM. There is nothing phony or fake about Me. I am Authentic. I don't play games and I don't wear masks. You can trust Me. Put all your trust in Me. It will never be misplaced and I will never let you down.

Sin makes people false and causes them to lose their innocence and honesty. I see and know the real you. I am aware of your every thought, word and deed. You can't pretend with Me or fool Me with smooth talk our phony worship. I desire and want a genuine relationship with you. Please don't play games with Me. It's impossible to fool Me. I know you have fallen often and fallen far and I know the reasons why. I see you when you are alone. I hear the stifled sob. I feel your loneliness and I know your fears. I love you. I care about you. My dear, dear child, remember what my son, Jesus said, "I have longed to gather you under my wings as a hen gathers her chicks, but, you would not let me!" Hold that image for a minute. I want to be close to you but sometimes you push Me away. Why? I will never harm you.

Come, come, and come – My dear beloved, unique, irreplaceable, precious child.

CHAPTER SEVEN

HELTER-SKELTER

Helter-skelter is disorganized haste. Speed is a component of helter-skelter but it is the state of disorganized speed that distinguishes it from normal speed. Our movements are hurried and jarred. We don't move at a healthy, normal, gentle pace; instead, we helter-skelter through life. What are we rushing away from and where are we rushing to?

I wish to emphasize "disorganized" haste. It is one thing to hurry when we need to but we dash here and there out of absoluter habit. Sometimes, we don't even know why we are hurrying. We are compulsive dashers. Recently, I observed a piece of concrete being removed from the base of a wall. I detected disorganized haste the minute the slab was pulled back. Bugs ran frantically in every direction. Ants removed eggs in hysterical haste whilst other insects dashed first in one direction then in another direction; not knowing which way to run. The scene resembled an aerial photo of a big city showing masses of people rushing to and fro; just like frantic ants.

There is a modern disease aptly called the hurry disease. It is due to haste addiction. We rush everywhere and we speed when there is no need for speed. Doing things at a normal, natural pace seems unnatural and boring. We sprint through breakfast, drive our cars too fast, eat our food at high-speed, talk quickly and move jerkily. Our vacations are stressful. We rush to our holiday destination and no sooner arrive than we gallop to the shops or beach. A holiday can be stress-loaded and agitation-packed! We argue and bicker. We simply don't know how to adjust when the pace of life slows down to an ordinary, natural pace. The pace feels unnatural - so we sprint to the nearest shop, restaurant or place of entertainment where we feel "more alive". We return home from holiday and wonder why we don't feel more relaxed and invigorated!

The hurry-disease is taking its toll on our mental, emotional and physical well-being because it is unnatural and unhealthy. We are NOT machines. We must learn to attune and align ourselves with the rhymes of our body and to nature. Observe free birds! They return to their nests at sunset and settle down for the night, then stir at sunrise and leisurely stretch their wings before they fly out of the nest. Contrast this to us humans - we awake in the morning, fly out of the bed and then spend the entire day dashing to and fro.

Battery hens are kept under perpetual artificial light in sheds. They are fed 24 hours a day, every day under electric light for the laying of more eggs. They no longer know day from night. Is this natural and humane? We tend to think we are more productive by routinely working late into the night but our bodies pay the price for this foolish, false productivity. Not only do we work late into the night but we also enjoy late-night entertainment. Somebody recently said to me, "We are not here on earth for a long time but for a good time!" Are we on earth simply to live short, frantic, pleasure-driven lives? Sadly, our children are learning this ridiculous, destructive lifestyle from us. Children speak too easily and often of being bored and constantly seek entertainment in order to be relieved from boredom. What happened to the days when children knew how to entertain themselves by playing in nature, riding bicycles, playing ball games in a street with their friends, jumping over ropes, playing hop-scotch, climbing hills, running in meadows? Now I watch the tiny fingers of toddlers playing with smartphone buttons or the television remote as they sit, engrossed by inanimate electronic gadgets. Their nervous and muscular systems need to be exercised through play and physical activities. Observe the animal kingdom as their offspring play and gambol most of the day and in so doing, develop their bodies and learn valuable survival and social skills! Children need to read books in order to stimulate their imaginations rather than watching games on the Xbox or television. Why tax the imagination when everything is right there in front of you on a screen? Obesity amongst children is a huge problem as a result of this sedentary lifestyle. Convenient fast foods, lack of exercise and physical activity are to blame for this malaise. There is a price to be paid and it is being paid now due to our helter- skelter lifestyle (if we dare call it a lifestyle!)

We don't know how to relax because it seems boring and a waste of time! We are like race horses with bits in our mouths waiting for the stall gate to open so we can burst forth and gallop away, but, unlike the race horse, we go helter-skelter with no clear goal in mind.

Serene and tranquil! They sound quaint and archaic don't they? How many calm (serene) people do you know? Are you serene? Are you tranquil? Do you know anyone who knows inner peace? Tranquil means to be free from agitation and to be undisturbed. Agitation is ubiquitous in our adrenalin-soaked populations. Certain types of people don't feel alive unless they are agitated. How can one become tranquil? It's not as simple or easy as simply deciding to be tranquil but rather a gradual process requiring patience. Weaning ourselves from the things that cause anxiety, agitation and that disturb our mental and emotional poise will have to be undertaken. The first step towards becoming tranquil is to stop and identify what the causes of agitation, anxiety and disturbance are. We can't free ourselves from what we don't have insight into. Unless we understand the triggers, we will continue to live life in mindless, perpetual motion just as a hamster in a wheel does. Our lives ARE busy but we need to ask if the busyness is the habit of going around in compulsive hurry-circles that, simply put, lead to an early grave?

We shop until we drop because we are brainwashed consumers. We are compelled to shop. Most of us can identify with the emotional rush we feel when we enter a mall or shop! The shelves are loaded with goods and advertisements encourage us to buy, buy, and buy. We think: "When I buy this, I will be SO happy!" We buy but then we have to pay for what we purchased and the emotional high wanes at the check-out. The thing we bought wasn't quite what we imagined it to be. It's what a drug addict feels when s/he experiences the let-down hell after the drug's effects recede! That's withdrawal! Then, off we go again and repeat the buying spree. Oh, the highs and lows of consumerism! Worse still, our children are modelling our shopping habits. Supermarkets are making children trolleys and if that isn't grooming children to become hooked consumers, then I don't know what is! Now mom and her ten year old child can push their separate trolleys and stock them together! We have to buy the necessities of life but so much of what we purchase has nothing to do with necessities. We are brainwashed via covert and overt suggestions via advertisements. We aren't called "consumers" for nothing. Much of what we buy ends up cluttering our wardrobes and cupboards. We spend more than we can afford to spend and the debt cycle is set in motion.

Turn-over is profit and things aren't made to last anymore. Businesses know that replacement is far more profitable than repair. Sometimes it costs more to repair an item than it does to replace it! The same applies to professions. The more people consulted; the faster the turn-over and, thus, profit made.

It doesn't make sense when a nation is urged to buy instead of save. Gone are the days when we were encouraged to save our money and receive fair rates of interest. Now we have to pay a bank when we deposit money in order to save it. I did calculations one day and found that it was costing me more to deposit my money in a bank, what with all the various charges etc., than the interest I was receiving. I wasn't making money but losing money by banking it! It's crazy! Today, we pay banks for doing what banks are supposed to do – be the custodian of public money. It is almost impossible nowadays to do business without a bank debit or credit card. Can one run a business today without having a bank account? We are in the bank/money trap! Money is no longer king and we are beholden to banks, nay, held hostage to banks. We are economically trapped by the banking industry due to electronics and cyber money. About ten years ago, I witnessed a bank manager supervising the day's deposits being placed in a huge safe - not so anymore. Our money isn't sitting snugly in a safe and you probably won't find a huge safe in a bank because money is now electronic, cyber money. A bank employee blithely informed me one day when I enquired why money that was due me hadn't been deposited into my account, "Oh, it is safe. It's floating about in cyber space being processed." Yikes! The reply was not comforting or reassuring at all!

Our machines are getting bigger and faster and use to await our dictates but now they dictate to us. I am tired of being called, beckoned to and alerted by mobile phones, kettles, microwave ovens, stoves and my laptop, remote door bells etc. I receive messages on my laptop that don't kindly request me to do certain things, it tells me – nay, commands me! For example, DO NOT POWER OFF MACHINE. DO NOT SWITCH-OFF. CONFIGURING. I don't know what configuring is! Modern cars, trains, planes, and computers are getting quicker and faster. How can we keep pace? Just when I think I am on par with something electronic; I discover it is obsolete and being replaced by something quicker, faster, and smarter.

How can nature compete with our electronics, technology and machines when we are taking more and more from the land, skies, rivers, seas and oceans – everything. We are literally dismantling our planet! Wild animals are being forced out from their natural habitation as we take more and more land away from them. We chop down huge, ancient trees in minutes due to our rapid-cutting machines. A tree that can take fifty, a hundred years, even a thousand years to grow to maturity can be reduced to planks and saw-dust in under an hour. Imagine that! Our helter-skelter rate of destroying nature is creating an inhospitable, uninhabitable planet. We must end this madness. It IS madness! Nature will not bow to the dictates of man. If we succeed in making our planet a wasteland, nature will survive and make a return but mankind will not survive. The grass and flowers will make a comeback, trees will grow but man will not be around to see or enjoy our planet again. Nature will have the last laugh. Bear in mind that plants were here before man was created and they will be here when man has gone. It is mankind's arrogance that causes him us to think that God intended humans to dominate over and dictate to everything on earth. The Creator instructed mankind to be earth's gardener; not its destroyer. Humans act as if they are the creator. Our planet does not belong to us; it belongs to the Creator. Mankind must keep reminding itself that God so loved the entire WORLD! Everything needs everything else and every living thing is inter-related, inter-dependent and inter-linked. The sooner we realize this; the better for us and our dear earth.

Nature teaches many lessons. There are some species of animal that live many, many years - some tortoises are over 100 years old. Lions, however, have relatively short lives. The oldest tree is usually the slowest growing tree. A tortoise is a slow creature and its movements are slow and unhurried. Perhaps this is the reason for its longevity unlike the relatively short life of lions who pace and sprint in sudden spurts. It is a fast animal powered by adrenalin. It seldom reaches old age. Modern man's life is restless, hurried and adrenalin-driven. Our adrenal glands are over-stimulated and exhausted. Is it any wonder we are dying from stress-induced and stress-related illnesses? We need to rediscover the body's natural pace and rhythm if we wish to be healthy and live to a vigorous, vital, old age. Dis-ease is disharmony throughout the entire body. Equilibrium and homeostasis are prerequisites for health and the maintenance of health. Excessive, prolonged haste and stress push the body's capacity to maintain balance to the edge, and, dis-ease is the result. I have heard the saying, "Drop Dead!!" We ARE dropping dead because we refuse to admit and acknowledge that we are not supermen/women. We are not robots but humans made of bone, blood, organs and tissue.

In our age of speed, the elderly and aged are regarded as being too slow. Younger generations get impatient with the "senior citizens": they walk too slowly, count their coins out at shop tills, spend ages putting their groceries into their shopping bags, shuffle on and off buses and so forth. Governments appear to be taking an unfavorable view of the aged and seem to be focusing their attention almost exclusively on the young. They are bemoaning the fact that their ageing populations are costing too much money. Modern medicine has made it possible for people to live longer but recently I have detected complaints against this medical marvel. This must set off alarm bells! I am already hearing, too frequently, of the elderly being neglected and abused in state-run homes. The way a country treats its most vulnerable citizens i.e. children, handicapped, elderly etc. reveals whether it is civilized and humane, or cruel and barbaric. Too many hospital beds are "blocked" by elderly patients for months; even years! Some families want to avoid the costs that will arise when the elderly family member is discharged and will need to be cared for at home or in an old-age home. To run an old-age home is an expensive business and the money must come from somewhere. Thus, when the aged one dies, the state claims from his/her estate in order to recoup the costs involved in caring for the person in the old-age home subsidized by the state. Some family members wish to avoid this happening or perhaps having to contribute towards the costs incurred by the state. Thus, elderly patients are left to languish in hospital as doctors cannot discharge them without them either being cared for by family members or placed in old-age homes. This morning I heard about such an elderly patient who has been in hospital for four years and who could have been discharged a few weeks after being admitted to hospital! Hospitals have morphed into hospital and old-age homes! Is it any wonder then that genuine patients have to lay on trollies in a corridor or in a cubicle for days because no beds in available in the wards? I don't begrudge the youth the focused concern and interest; but not at the expense of the elderly. The elderly made their contribution to society - let no state forget that. Remind the youth of that. The roads, bridges, tunnels and cities that we enjoy today didn't just materialize. These are the fruits of those who were once young and vigorous.

The young are quick in everything and slow in patience. They can't imagine themselves other than being young and think getting old will never happen to them. For them, old age is a far distant country. It doesn't feel that long ago that I felt Forever Young but the years came and went and youth is fleeting. The elderly teach us valuable lessons and show that there is a saner pace to life and living. On the whole, the elderly are gentle and kind and have little desire to amass, dominate or control. They reconnect to nature and take nothing and no one for granted. Our senior citizens have learned many life lessons, experienced many losses and endured many heart aches. They fell time and time again but got up each time. They have survived life's steepest mountains and deepest valleys. As they inch towards the sunset of life, they tend to incline themselves more to the Beloved and peer ahead with hope and expectation to that fairer shore and of being reunited again with their loved ones. Life, for them, has become a glowing ember – a setting sun.

Don't think that old age is golden for everyone for there are numberless who suffer from many troubles i.e. money insecurity, arthritis, dodgy memory, loss of hearing, diminishing eyesight and many other age-related maladies. I used to look at a drawing of a silver-haired woman knitting away with a beautified smile of content on her face and her rosy-cheeked husband puffing away on his pipe reading his newspaper in front of roasting fire. Not an ache or pain! Blithely and ignorantly, I imagined that the picture epitomized the golden years but the truly golden years are the young adult years when we are at the peak of physical health and vitality; surrounded by family members and friends and with a steady, secure job. To reach old age is an achievement when you consider how much a person has to experience and endure to reach it. Not all are so fortunate!

The helter-skelter syndrome has affected and infected many professions. Quick turn-over is quick money. The more time spent with one client; the more money wasted. Sadly, this is affecting the medical profession.

Doctors don't make house calls anymore because it is too time-consuming and money-losing. Let the patient come to the doctor. Cities are expanding rapidly and becoming busier and busier and a doctor can no longer go to a patient's home as in bygone days. Patients are now wedged into 15 minutes time-slots! The medical profession has had to adapt to changing times but the pendulum has swung too far from one extreme to the other.

We have become dehumanized and are no longer people but numbers, codes, passwords and PINS and we won't get far by using our name anymore and must produce our membership number, card, PIN and so forth ad infinitum. We are just information on a program in a computer! Thank Goodness that there are still a few pockets of small businesses that recognize one by face and name and long may they flourish and multiply! Recently, I was obliged to complete a lengthy application form and was requested to answer ALL the questions in block letters and in black pen! There were so many questions and some were of a personal nature and I wouldn't have been surprised if I was requested to submit my dental records, urine sample, DNA and my entire family tree!

Worship has become boring and ponderous. We are speed and haste addicts and to sit in a church and listen to a sermon taxes our endurance to the limit. We want excitement and entertainment. Some ministers have tried to pep-up their services in order to retain a congregation; or gain one. We have so much to do and going to church is a waste of precious and valuable time. Simply put - we don't have time for God. The Beloved, churches and worshipping are oh-so boring! Not long ago, a mass was shortened due to the fact that the congregation wanted to watch an international sport match on television!

It is difficult for religion to appeal to the youth today as churches have not kept pace with the changing times. The Holy Message is timeless but religions have not applied it to a rapidly changing world. Women too will no longer; and, rightly so, accept being regarded as less valuable, less important than or less equal to men. They are tired of being blamed for the big fall, resultant woes in the world, fed-up with being dominated and being regarded as the weaker sex. How ridiculous, pompous and arrogant for an all-male church council to decide about birth control, contraception and family rights and duties? Religion has been/is cruel, unkind and unfair to women. Women are NOT property - God made men and women equal.

Man decided to declare them unequal! Christianity has failed both youth and women. If Christianity is to become robust and relevant again; it will have to be overhauled. If it doesn't; it will continue to decline and other religions will willingly fill the vacuum vacated by it.

God won't be hurried and has all the time in eternity for He is timeless. The Beloved is immortal but we are mortal and bound and restrained by space and time. A thousand years is like a day to God. He knows nothing of helter-skelter and to Him there are no such things as haste or disorganization. Nothing about God is disorganized. A baby takes nine months to develop in the womb before it is ready to make its entrance and when the time is ripe; it will let the mom know. Every cell knows what it is destined to become and from one ovum and one sperm emerges a complex being of unimagined organization. We can't comprehend or imagine the Almighty. The Creator has chosen to love us and He bears in mind that we are made of dust. Our bodies are so extraordinary and yet so fragile! Like the wild flower; we take root, grow, flourish, wither and die. How thankful we ought to be that He remembers we are fragile beings, living on the shell of a medium-sized planet with a molten core at its center, revolving around a medium-size star in one galaxy amongst billions of other galaxies. Please make time for God! Be grateful that He makes time for you and is never too busy for you.

Coo'ee My dear one,

I AM! Do you know what this means? It means I am eternal, immortal and UNCHANEABLE. Nothing can be added or subtracted from Me. I AM complete and cannot be changed, altered or modified!

Change is everywhere but not all change is progress. Progress without wisdom is dangerous and foolish. Man is hurrying and he doesn't stop to consider the consequences of his actions. Pause and recall My words, "BE still and know that I AM God." It is one thing to know about Me but I want you to know Me. There is a life-changing difference.

When you go to a graveyard; stop and read the inscriptions on some of the tombstones. Most have the person's names, a few words and the person's date of birth and death. In the past, when life wasn't so hurried; people used to engrave the date of birth and death in full i.e. born 21

September 1960 Died 5 March 2016 and added a few words that gave in inkling of who the person was but these days you are more likely to see the dates shortened to *21/9/1960 - + 5/3/2016! The * signifying birth and + signifying death. Even grave inscriptions have not escaped the rush-pace of modern man! It is ironic that man's life is now a dash between the date of birth and the moment of death. How sad! I desire My loved ones to live full lives full of life! Man is rushing from the womb to the tomb. Why?

My dear one, no matter how much or how far man progresses; he can never progress beyond Me. Remember the men of old who built the tower of Babel? They thought they could build a tower high enough to reach Me! I AM not a destination out there somewhere. I AM within. They thought they could build a God-scraper! The tower crashed down in a heap of stone and rubble. How foolish and, yet, man is still trying to reach Me or proof My existence through progress. Why doesn't man look within himself? He will find Me if he looks with humility and sincerity.

Slow down My child. Think of what makes life worthwhile. Stop and think. Spend time with things that really matter. I matter - I should matter. Do you want to fritter away your life in trivial pursuit until the day you die? It is too late then to realize that dashing from womb to the tomb is a waste of precious time! Life is too precious and short to play silly games.

I AM the only true constant. Trust Me. Believe Me. Have you ever stopped to consider how much I trust you? I trusted you with; life, potential, talent and with so much besides. I trusted the world when I sent My beloved, Jesus, and look what it did to Him! They tortured and crucified Him! I ask you, has there ever been a more fulfilled life than His? He lived for only thirty-three years on earth but what thirty-three years they were! No inscription on a tomb could ever capture the fullness of the life He lived or His being!

My child, don't live the abbreviated helter-skelter life. Live the full life that only I can give. I will fill your cup to overflowing if you choose the life I am offering you this very minute.

CHAPTER EIGHT

GODXIT

In June 2016, Britain held a referendum to remain in or exit the EU. The majority voted in favor of leaving the EU and Brexit became a reality. It came as a huge shock to the world as most thought Britain would choose to retain its membership and benefits. The pound sterling plunged in value and stock markets were turbulent as investors and companies sold their British based shares. David Cameron resigned. The Labor Party is splitting. Scotland is in an uproar as the majority of its people voted to remain in the EU. Theresa May is Britain's new Prime Minister, and, what an unenviable task she faces. Boris Johnson, who championed Brexit, was appointed Foreign Minister!

The USA is facing uncertain times. A new president was elected and Donald Trump was sworn-in on 20th January 2017. Yes, we are living in turbulent, unsettled, uncertain times!

The EU leadership told Britain that it must trigger Article 50 to set in motion the dismantling of its membership and it will wait until it does. In the meantime, members of the EU convene and meet without a British representative. There are now fears that other EU countries may contemplate separating from the EU too.

There is disquiet and displeasure regarding the EU's apparent indecisiveness and lack of action regarding urgent matters assailing Europe. Illegal migrants are pouring into Europe almost hourly and the EU leaders appear clueless about how to stem the inflow, resulting in ever-increasing numbers arriving on Europe's shores. Mass illegal migration to Europe is viewed as the second biggest threat to its economy and it will soon be confronted by another, looming crises of biblical proportions. It is estimated that 20 million people face starvation in Nigeria, South Sudan, Somalia and Yemen. The shocking and disturbing fact is that the famines are manmade! Civil wars have raged for many years in these countries. Europe is facing unprecedented mass migration to its shores as a result of the instability in these countries.

The civil war in Syria is uprooting and displacing millions of Syrians and many are streaming into Europe. Why is the UN impotent regarding Bashar al-Assad? Meeting, after meeting, is arranged by the EU to discuss world crises but little emerges after all the jaw-jawing. Europeans are restless and angry at the inability and lack of will by the EU's leaders to collectively agree on minor and major issues. People want more action, fewer conferences and less talking. Many EU member countries feel their national and domestic affairs are being dictated to from Brussels.

Many British voted to leave the EU because they want the "old" England and "old" English way of life and living back. They don't like today's "new" England and its indistinct, diluted identity. It's difficult to recognize the remnants of the old England. It no longer exists. Can it be regained? The hands of the clock cannot be turned back. Wishing to return to the "old" England is easy but it is an unrealistic dream for time has moved on and the world has changed. People are migrating world-wide. Societies are multi-cultural, multi-religious and multi-racial. The tolerance of nations is taxed when immigrants and migrants demand their national, cultural and religious rights and privileges which are contrary to and which impinge on the adopted country's customs and way of life. There is no such thing anymore as Mexico for the Mexicans, Africa for the Africans, Arabia for Arabs, Russia for Russians, Indians for Indians, America for American and Europe for the Europeans etc.

People have always moved to different parts of the globe but the problem today is the scale of mass migration to specific parts of the world. The world's populations are splintering and splitting. As the world's population keeps expanding, the demand for employment increases and as migrants keep migrating, is it any wonder that citizens of a country want to recapture or retain their identity, culture and way of life? Xenophobia is an escalating problem. The world is too small for mankind's ever-burgeoning population and, unfortunately, the poorest countries tend to have the highest birth rates.

It is natural for the truly desperate to make their way to countries that have more to offer them than their own country does. Is it right though that Europe, Canada, USA and Australia shoulder the burden of mass illegal migration when the true cause of much of the migration is often due to incompetent, corrupt and immoral government leaders and officials who loot their country's purse through squandering, plundering, nepotism and theft?.

Many years ago, when Ethiopia was experiencing a long and devastating drought, I observed a scene on television that I have never forgotten. Rivers were dry. Cattle were dying. People were dying. There was one stream of flowing water in a river and people came in their droves with containers. In no time at all, the water stopped flowing and the river dried up. When the economic and food "streams" of a country dry up because they are over-taxed; economic famine is inevitable. The desperate migrate to counties whose economic streams are "flowing". The solution is to keep the streams of economy flowing in each country in the world! The remedy is for each country to conserve and grow its economy so that the proceeds flow where they are most needed and not into foreign bank accounts of corrupt, greedy politicians. The world has only so many "streams" of employment, health care, schools, hospitals, clinics etc. As we consume more and more of the world's natural resources and destroy its food-producing ability, so the demand for food and raw materials will increase. The earth's resources will decrease to a trickle, like the river in Ethiopia, and the end result will be large-scale drought and famine.

Is it not strange that world leaders are not declaring that over-population of the world is unsustainable and one of the biggest, urgent problems facing mankind? The planet is suffocating due to over-population. Imagine earth is a medium-size pizza. How many slices of pizza can be cut? If we try to feed a thousand people with a single pizza; each person will get, at most, crumbs. It's ridiculous! Again, imagine that a country is the size of medium-sized ferry and afloat. Now, try to imagine what will happen if thousands of people clamber aboard - it will either capsize or sink! Likewise, first world countries are sinking under the financial and social weight of the never-ending inflow of illegal migrants. I have read of ferries capsizing and sinking because they were over-loaded. The ferry was never designed to carry such excess weight but designed to carry a limited, safe weight in order to be stable and stay afloat. Earth is barely afloat due to being swamped and over-loaded. It is tilting alarmingly. Earth was never designed or meant to carry such already over-sized populations and it is beyond credulity that it continues to expand at an explosive rate! Many thought the Titanic was unsinkable. It sank on its maiden voyage. Unless we change our thinking; the earth will sink! The earth is not unsinkable! We are already at the critical point of global warming and the last three years have been the hottest in recorded history. It will be too late to reverse the process when we reach the point-of-no-return. We are now experiencing the consequences of the accumulation of hundreds of years of man pumping carbon dioxide and other toxic gases into the atmosphere. There is no happy ever-after, no fairytale ending and neither do we have the luxury of a nearby, spare planet! We have opened the forbidden Pandora box and removed the lid. Not only have we removed it, but we lost it! Hopefully, mankind will soon remember where he lost it and replace it firmly back into place where it belongs.

What is nonsensical is the fact that countries are accepting illegal migrants whilst many of their own citizens go homeless, hungry, unemployed and sick! These are refugees in the country of their birth! I recently saw footage on television of bedraggled people in a certain European city holding placards saying, "Refugee in my own country. I have no other country I can go to!" Charity starts at home. There are reports that refugees are given furnished accommodation, free medical, free schooling, etc.! I DO NOT begrudge GENUINE refugees kindness and assistance, but why aren't the needy and desperate in their country of birth not given the same generosity and assistance by their government? Just why is this? Does anyone wish to explain?

Many people have lost their home because of retrenchment. Businesses have down-sized and laid-off staff and many have gone into liquidation or filed for bankruptcy. No one wants to be homeless! Governments must assist their citizens who have become economic refugees through no fault of their own. The number of homeless people seeking assistance is at an all-time high and the need for houses is greater than it has been in many years yet citizens aren't given the same privileges as refugees! Some homeless people are homeless because they are mentally ill and governments are failing them miserably. These "unfortunates" have nowhere to go and end up roaming the streets and living on the streets! Instead of providing assistance and appropriate accommodation for the mentally ill; they are literally dumped onto the streets! Surely, western and so-called first-world countries ought to take care of its genuine and truly desperate citizens!

If only ALL the countries of the world are as generous and humane when it comes to accepting genuine refugees and asylum seekers! Turkey and a few others middle-eastern countries are doing much, however, can't countries such as Saudi Arabia, Bahrain, Qatar and Oman do more? Kenya is doing much, but why is Africa not doing more? Why are China and India not doing more? Why are these countries so conveniently silent?

South Africa is in turmoil. Many buildings built during the colonial period are being burnt to the ground – including libraries and railway stations. The economy of South Africa is so bad that 16 South African Rands is worth 1 Euro! This morning I saw a photograph of a shell of a building. It once stood on a very productive farm that produced enough oranges and mangoes to supply South Africa and had enough over to export the surplus overseas. The farm was handed over in a "Land Redistribution" deal. All the fruit trees withered and died – not from drought but from apathy. The equipment was stripped and sold. President Zuma recently fired a competent minister of Finance and re-shuffled his cabinet resulting in the ZA Rand plummeting further in value. He has replaced a competent Minister of Finance with an inexperienced minister! Is this yet another case of nepotism? Zimbabwe is in even worse condition. The value of the Zimbabwe dollar today is 100 ZWD = 0.26068 Euro! It used to be a bread-basket country that exported goods and food. Robert Mugabe has been president since 1980! Zimbabwe is facing famine and its baskets are empty! The country is in shambles but Mugabe still manages to jet to Asia for medical treatment! Too many African leaders have been in power for far too long. They vehemently resist being replaced or ousted! Gambia is a recent example. Some leaders act as if they have a divine right to rule as long as they draw breath and the right to bequeath leadership to their family as an inheritance. Too many tin-pot dictators live in the lap of luxury, are tended to in overseas hospitals when ill whilst their citizens starve, live in shanties and have little to no access to health care.

Many of the comments I hear over the radio concerning Donald Trump are sarcastic and negative. The transparent dislike and disdain of him is repeated, day-after-day. With anti-Trump mania in full-swing, I have to question why journalists haven't been as vociferous about other world leaders! Can it be that the concentrated anti-Trump-mania is a diversion ploy to draw attention away from domestic problems that are shocking and embarrassing - some in the very countries that denounce Trump so self-righteously? He hasn't been in power long and perhaps the world should give him time to settle in. Much of what I saw on television on the 21st January 2017 in so-called "peaceful" protests against Trump was sheer hooliganism. It isn't necessary to smash windows and vandalize property to vent personal views and opposition. It's was yet another excuse for thuggery.

Let's consider the knee-jerk reaction of the USA post the Twin Towers attack! In a bid to show the USA muscle and to deflect the horror, embarrassment and insult of what had been inflicted, America and its ally, Britain, destabilized the entire Middle East by attacking Iraq. No evidence of weapons of mass destruction was found by the UN inspectors prior to the decision to invade Iraq. Saddam Hussein was captured and executed. Gadhafi was captured and executed in Libya. Operation Desert Storm had consequences that neither the USA nor Britain foresaw. Egypt was plunged into turmoil. The USA and Britain withdrew their troops and today the world is more unstable and insecure as a result of their shortsighted decision to invade Iraq. Osama Bin Laden was eventually hunted down and executed. Syria is at war with itself and Yemen is under attack. Turkey faces huge challenges. Forces are marching towards Mosul in order to reclaim it from Isis. Isis became a power due to the destabilization of Iraq plus Libya and the consequential power vacuum that was created. Much of the modern, sophisticated western military equipment was left behind and one can only surmise whose hands they are in now.

As already stated, my heart goes go out to genuine refugees and asylum-seekers but world leaders must apply pressure on those who create chaos, destruction and in-fighting rather than simply take the passive, lazy route of opening borders and doors to fleeing masses. There is a vast distinction between migrants and refugees and asylum seekers. Europe is being invaded by illegal migrants - they are NOT refugees. When these migrants arrive, many of them blend into the shadows and are not registered or finger-printed. Why is this onslaught of illegal migrants not being addressed? There was a time when a distinction was made between refugees/asylum seekers and migrants but now I only hear the term of refugee used. These illegal migrants come, daily, in their thousands. The message they and the people smugglers get is that the EU is dithering, unwilling or incapable of preventing them from reaching Europe. Why is the EU and the UN not putting an end to this? If Europe was being invaded by a hostile country right now, it would, hopefully, mobilize and defend itself. Europe IS being invaded and it is not putting up much of a defense!

Recently, on television, I watched people smugglers on the side of a busy road in France. They were not afraid of being seen or filmed. They lined up illegal migrants along the road, awaiting an opportunity to jump into large trucks when the trucks stopped because the smugglers had chopped down trees and dragged them across the road! One such smuggler had a long stick and started beating a migrant because he had not paid the fee for being smuggled into France! He was not deterred from hitting the man because he knew there would few, if any, repercussions! When the police finally arrived, the smugglers and migrants slinked back into the dark shadows to await their next opportunity.

In December 2016, a Libyan deliberately drove a huge truck into pedestrians in Berlin. It resulted in the death of at least nine people and inflicted life-altering injuries to many of his victims. The culprit was known to have terrorist links and was facing deportation but the deportation process was slow. He managed to travel from Germany to Italy on public transport, thanks to Europe being borderless! He almost escaped to North Africa before spotted, shot and killed. Nice and Stockholm have experienced similar attacks. A borderless Europe is a terrorist's dream come true!

A few days ago, there was a knock on my front door. A young woman stood before me. She was appealing for donations on behalf of UNICEF who was asking for donations for Aleppo and I admired her ardor. Innocent, suffering people in Aleppo are in dire need but aren't there ever-increasing numbers of homeless people in Europe who are also in dire need of assistance? Families with children live in hotel rooms or hostels because they are homeless and the rooms/cubicles are small with nowhere to wash clothes or dry them. The children have nowhere to play.

These citizens are refugees too for they are the victims of an economic war. A vacant building was occupied by desperate people because of the indignities they experienced in hostels provided by the council. Some families, with children, have to share space with drug addicts who openly use drugs in the hostel!

Hospitals and schools can't cope in some European countries due to the lack of funding and the ever-increasing numbers of patients/scholars. Some people have to lay on trolleys in corridors for up to three days before being admitted to a bed in a ward – many of them in their seventies and older! The Red Cross has called today's state of health care in England: "A humanitarian crises!" There is talk now that Britain is considering supplying drug addicts with free drugs in an attempt to prevent death by overdosing and to wean them off drugs. Part of the decision is because paramedics are daily called out to attend to addicts who have overdosed resulting in ambulances and hospital services being put under added pressure and stress. I am not sure how much it is going to cost the NHS (approx. 3 thousand pounds per addict, per month?)

People who have to languish on a trolley in a hospital for hours or days are exposed to noise, bright lights and have no privacy. It is a form of unintentional torture. In wars, prisoners were tortured by bombarded of noise and light and now hospitals are becoming like war zones. Despite the urgent and overwhelming problems facing European countries, the EU leadership continues to stipulate that member states must take their quota of refugees AND migrants.

There is not ONE animal to be seen on any film footage taken in the war-torn countries in Syria - not one! I have not seen a dog, cat, horse, donkey or a camel but I saw many resemblances of buildings that look like rotten teeth - stumps. Neither have I seen birds or trees. What happened to the animals, birds and trees? The fact that they are not mentioned or shown at all shows that they are regarded as collateral damage and of little importance or consequence. Update: On television last night, I was heartened to see an animal rescue organization attending to animals in Mosul's zoo. The animals were a pitiful sight; having suffered trauma and starvation. A magnificent lion and bear are to be relocated to safer countries, and, hopefully, the other animals in the zoo will also be rescued and relocated.

I heard over the radio that all humanitarian aid intended for Aleppo could not be delivered due to yet ANOTHER failed truce and cease-fire. Many of the donated provisions and food are stolen. An ancient Roman amphitheater and an equally ancient Roman statue in Palmyra have either been destroyed or irreparably damaged by Isis. Isis had previously destroyed the ancient buildings and statues in Palmyra whilst the rest of the world tut-tutted its dismay. Forces recaptured Palmyra from Isis but now have lost it again to Isis!

Why are there so few women refugees/asylum-seekers/migrants in comparison to men refugees/ asylum-seekers/migrants? I heard recently that an EU country has leased a four-star hotel, complete with swimming pool, as a processing center for refugees! It has allocated millions of Euros for the welfare of 200 refugees! How does a government explain this when many of its citizens struggle to make ends meet? Twenty "under-18?" unaccompanied males from the once-sprawling refugee camp outside Calais in France, will be accommodated in the four-star hotel processing center and receive free medical treatment for their various ailments by top specialists. Are they genuine refugees? No wonder citizens are becoming restless and angry. What will it take to kick-start the EU and UN into action?

Whenever I see television footage of parliaments in session, be it in South Africa or Europe, I notice the numerous empty seats! There are fewer present than there are absent! I am constantly amazed by this and also by how often parliaments go into recess! There are also, believe it or not, occasions when motions can't be passed because there aren't enough members of parliament present to form a quorum!

Here's a little parable: "Once there was a man who had seven children. All went well during the "boom" years and no one lacked anything. Then a huge drought occurred and it was a calamity. Gone were the years of easy plenty. Soon a famine stalked the land and one by one his children withered away and lost their strength. A strong wind arose and tore down their houses. They were hungry and cold. Only the father's house stood standing. The father had a few sheep and some pots of fresh water. A war broke out in a faraway country and houses were razed to the ground, all the cattle and sheep were stolen and the people were in want. They heard about the man in a faraway land whose house still stood, who had some sheep and a few pots of water so they all decided to go to him for assistance. Off they went. In the meantime, the weakest of the father's sons came to him and said: "Father, I am in desperate want. Open your door to me and let me in and quench my parched tongue and assuage my hunger pangs." But, the father replied, "Go forth son and, perchance, you may find shelter, a morsel to eat and a cup of water but I must give my best room, best portion of meat and the coolest water to a stranger lest my neighbors consider me uncharitable." Broken in spirit, the son left his father's door and entered the barren wilderness. In the meantime, the strangers from the faraway land arrived at the man's door and he smiled, opened the door wide and said, "Come in, come in. My house is your house. Abide between my walls. Eat my meat and drink my water for I am a good man and, indeed, a good neighbor." And they did as he bade them do. Now my friends – what do you think of such a father?

There is rumbling discontent in Europe and people are disillusioned. There is growing impatience as Europe seems to be groping in the dark without any sense of direction. Europe's governments and the EU leadership would be wise to take note and listen. Like Nero who played the fiddle whilst Rome burned, the EU and the UN leadership is fiddling with endless meetings and pointless conferences whilst Europe's populations are burning with impatience and anger.

The world immediately reacted when it heard that Britain had voted to exit the EU. Boris Johnson resigned, David Cameron resigned and Nigel Farage resigned. Global stock markets reacted and the British pound slumped in value. How did the world react when Jesus was murdered? Did stock markets get the jitters? Did the US dollar devalue overnight? Did Pontius Pilate and Caiaphas resign? Of course not! It hardly caused a ripple!

Does the world conduct itself as if it believes in the existence of God? There were times it did. Mankind had fragmentary images of whom or what it believed God is. Some believed there were many gods but most viewed these gods as being far removed from mankind; often cruel and demanding sacrifice. These had to be appeased and played with puny man - fear of and obedience was encouraged and expected. Gods were national deities and wars were waged to protect their honor. Ancient people believed in higher powers and deities and feared and respected them whereas today we laugh at the mere idea of a supreme being – God. Ah, modern man is far too sophisticated and suave to believe in God.

No referendum was carried out around the world recently to vote on continuing to retain our union with God. If only it was that obvious. Apparently, the decision to Godexit was made by others on our behalf. The West decided to separate from God. Modern man no longer looks to the Creator for guidance or leadership and have chosen to put our trust in our modern-day golden calves of economy, trade, electronics and technology - things that we can see and touch. The 21ˢᵗ century has grown tired of waiting for God and we are an impatient, impetuous people. Our spiritual leaders have been silent and absent from our camp and we are heading towards an Unpromising Land! The future is unclear, uncertain and appears more like a Punishing Land than a Promised Land. We gather around our golden calf and forget the good, bygone days when we actually believed in God and the way life was back in old Eden.

Have you noticed how silent the Christian leaders are? Where are their outcries regarding the killing of innocent people in Europe by religious extremists and fanatics? Why aren't we hearing from the Christian leadership? Bar a few papal announcements, one would not be surprised to learn that all of them have suddenly been struck mute! Why no protestation or uproar when Christian customs, celebrations and events are being swept under the "political correctness" carpet? Tomorrow will be Good Friday but it will pass quietly due to almost everything in the West being reduced to bland uniformity in the feeble excuse of not wishing to offend! I am NOT a Christian fanatic and oppose domination by force and coercion by one religion against another however, it is blatantly obvious that Christianity is being targeted for deliberate marginalization and diminishment. Why don't we hear about the imprisonment, torture and death of Christians in some middle-eastern countries, India and Africa? The UN is impotent and toothless. It meets, confers, discusses and releases statements. The UN is a house-divided. Vladimir Putin shows his disdain for it by ignoring it and occasionally using the veto to block decisions. Truth be told, no person, leader or world organization knows how to resolve the many crises facing the world.

I watched arson attacks recently on television. In America, Australia and elsewhere, arsonists set fire to forests and vegetation simultaneously at various sites and the end-result was infernos that combined into one huge unstoppable blaze that consumed everything in its path. The destruction was horrific. All over the world there are small, big and huge conflicts breaking out and leaders and world organizations don't know where to start to bring them under control or how to control them. They no sooner bring one conflict under control than another takes spark somewhere else. If they don't succeed in bringing these global conflicts under control soon, they can and will merge and grow into a global conflagration.

The West is exiting from God. We are politically-correct but faith-incorrect! Christianity has been rendered weak. We bend over backwards to appease other religions and cultures who have chosen to live in the west. Why are we demanding that Europe become secular? Why is the West apologizing for its Christian faith! Europe is becoming diverse but that doesn't mean Western Europe must abandon Christianity! Why do we feel compelled to placate and appease followers of other religions? To appear politically incorrect is the new mortal sin! Why can't ALL people embrace their own beliefs and chosen religions? Why is there not the same level of tolerance and accommodation in other countries regarding Christians and the Christian faith?

Western governments appeased Hitler until he became so emboldened that he invaded Poland and the 2nd World War was the result! The West must assume some responsibility for Hitler's expansion of power and domination in Europe. If it had acted more decisively, the invasion of Europe and the Holocaust may never have happened! Their weakness and bumbling indecision helped shape Hitler into an egotistical megalomaniac! The West, today, is again appeasing and placating. What narcissistic megalomaniacs are we creating now through indecision and endless jaw-jawing? The church must also assume its share of responsibility for this sad state of affairs. We have been shocked by the extent of neglect, inhumane labor practices, extortion and physical and sexual abuse committed by some priests and nuns. These include pedophilic acts committed against children on an ongoing and horrific scale. Add to this tale of shame the covering-up and covering-over by those in power who knew of these abuses yet did nothing to stop the violators or remove them from office. Some of the offenders were merely shipped off to other parishes where they continued to molest children. Many have lost faith in Christianity due to this inexcusable, evil behavior. HOWEVER, NOT ALL the priests, ministers etc. were child molesters. Countless priests and ministers have been and are the light and salt of the earth and made/make differences and huge contributions to millions of lives, organizations and countries. And, do we honestly think that other religions have not been tainted by similar abhorrent behavior? We make an ENORMOUS mistake when we judge God by human institutions and human beings!

Children make a pledge to their country, hand over heart, and yet they are not allowed to pray in school! The West is stripping God from the curriculum and assemblies in its schools. The clamor is for secular schools. Thus, in part, is due to the church over-reaching its power and influence. Schools were hijacked to further the dominance of the church. But, nature abhors a vacuum and we must question what is filling the place and space that was once given to God and prayer. Christmas and other Christian special days and celebrations aren't practiced anymore in some schools yet other religions are allowed to practice theirs special days and celebrations. This is one-sided and discriminatory! Imagine my reaction when a radio announcer stated recently that consideration is being given to the display of an image of the crucified Christ as it may traumatize children! It is a traumatizing image! I'm sure Jesus was traumatized by being tortured and nailed to a cross! Most Protestant churches tend to only have the bare, bland cross on display. This is the sanitized version of the cross of Jesus! Maybe it is a symbol of the resurrection of Jesus? Maybe we should be reminded of man's cruelty to man (and Jesus)! The holocaust is recalled and remembered as are those who have fallen during the first and second world wars so why can't the death of Jesus be recalled and remembered? Who is considering a display of the crucified Jesus as being too traumatic for display? Just who are these anonymous people? This, in a world where children are killing other children and where many children are traumatized by bullies in school! Watching the news on television is truly traumatizing – even for adults! Mark my words; it won't be long before crucifixes and other symbols are removed from churches and replaced by sanitized, bland and neutral images instead. Last week I took a child to the library and asked the librarian for a well-known children's book so I could read it to Lucy. Imagine my shock when I was informed that the entire series of books I requested was no longer in the library due to their "dubious" content! Again, who decided this? This was censorship of delightful children stories whilst pornography is broadcast on television during family time and bare-breasted women adorn many a page in the daily tabloids! I don't even want to imagine what goes on in the minds of those who decided on the censorship of books depicting a little fellow wearing a long, red cap that has a silver bell attached to it!

In the West, other faiths and religions are opening and operating schools solely under the guidance and governance of a religious leader and exclusively for children of that faith. Their beliefs and customs are taught and inculcated in the schools. I don't deny them the privilege. Over time, Christianity will be replaced in the West as we are hell-bent on making state schools and society exclusively secular. I am NOT opposed to different religions and beliefs. I am not God. I do believe in Jesus Christ. Only God knows the heart and mind of every person. The Almighty judges - not me. Heaven may prove a big surprise and shock to those who believe that only certain, particular people will enter Heaven! Many considered unworthy by others may be considered worthy by God. It is not religion that grants us admission into God's kingdom. A belief in a loving, forgiving, compassionate and merciful God should make us better, kinder people. A genuine relationship with the Beloved must reveal itself in the fruits of love and service devoid of discrimination to all.

Gone are the days of grand cathedrals and churches wherein crowds attended services. Great was my astonishment when I saw a beautiful, old cathedral turned into a restaurant! The contrast was startling. It just didn't feel right. Disused and under-utilized churches in bulging cities are sought after. These were erected years ago when towns and cities were much smaller and now they occupy prime locations. Standing mostly vacant, they are being sold so that yet another mall, office block, apartments, garages or parking lots can be built where they once proudly stood.

God has always been used as a weapon and an excuse to engage in war and is still being so used today. It is blasphemous! God is portrayed as a god who takes sides and who helps a group or nation to win wars and destroy enemies. Why, I saw a boxer get on his knees the other day before a match and pray to God to help him win the fight! The crusaders went to the Holy Land and killed Muslims in God's name and then the Muslims returned the favor and killed the Christians. The burning of witches in

England and America was done in God's name! Jews were slaughtered in pogroms in numerous (Christian!) European countries -the Inquisition too was carried out in His name! Many a Christian priest and minister terrified people with graphic sermons of hell and damnation as punishment from God and frightened them into submission and a private hatred for such a God. Who can blame them?

Spiritual fear is a powerful weapon. Is it any wonder that God is disliked and misunderstood? Not only Christians misuse and abuse God. Innocent people were shot and killed in Paris and passengers at an airport in Belgium were murdered. People have been beheaded by religious extremists in the name of God! This is religious insanity! We have ONE Creator. The human race is ONE family. Torture and murder are the antithesis of what God is or what He desires.

The Cold War is over and we are now in The Scorching War that can bubble over at any moment into the 3rd World War! Nations are splitting into political and religious camps. True, many forms of discrimination have been overcome or are in the process of being overcome, however, religious and gender discrimination are on the increase. Armageddon will not be a battle pitted between good and evil but the desire to enforce a particular belief and religion on the world. Religious fanaticism can and may trigger World War 3!

Britain will leave the EU. Adam and Eve left the Garden of Eden. Both departures are due to decided and deliberate actions. God never left mankind - He never existed. The Beloved is ever-present. We decided to go it alone. When Adam and Eve left the garden they entered a wasteland and nothing was the same again. They lost the Garden of Eden for they declared their independence from God. The Almighty never triggered article 50 on us! He entered a covenant us and is committed to it. The EU is waiting for Britain to trigger article 50 and Britain must set the disengaging of ties in motion. God has never disengaged Himself from us - although we often disengage ourselves from Him. We often violate the terms of the covenant but the Beloved continually sent emissaries to us to remind us of His love for us. We showed our gratitude by silencing them. Not One to give up, He sent Jesus. There has never, nor, will there ever again be an Emissary like Him.

Why does the West try so hard to discredit Jesus? The West is parched and dying, yet it refuses to go to the oasis and drink its life-giving water. Angels spoke of Good News…. and, Oh, how the world needs to hear good news! We can do with less bad news that instills anxiety and fear. Jesus spoke of God as his Abba (Father) and God is also our Father. Jesus asked us to love God, ourselves and each other and urged unity. He unveiled a generous Father whose kindness knows no bounds or limits. When we mistreat or kill ANY living thing; we diminish, injure, and maltreat ourselves! A murderer not only kills another person but also something deep within himself. It cannot be otherwise.

God deserves respect. When He spoke to Moses, Moses was ordered to take off his sandals out of respect. All land is holy and all life is holy. The root cause of incivility and barbaric behavior today is because we have lost respect for God! If we can't/don't respect the Almighty; what can we respect? There is no reason to respect a God we don't believe exists! Lawlessness and cruelty are steeped in disrespect and the refusal to assume responsibility or be held accountable.

Once Britain triggers article 50 there will be no way back for it to re-join the EU - there will be no second chances or change of heart tolerated. Theresa May has announced that the UK will opt for a hard-exit from the EU. In like-manner, many have opted for a hard-exit from God! Fortunately, God has not hard-exited from us and has no desire to separate from us. The Beloved counsels us to carefully reconsider our decision to go it alone and to disengage from Him. His door is an open door. He has given us free will and will not force or implore us to enter. The EU (Eternal Union) with God is an open invitation and all it requires is our acceptance. God gives us many opportunities to turn to Him and enter into a loving relationship with Him. This is the God of second chances and changes of heart! Your Creator awaits your decision.

Coo'ee My dear one,

Since Adam and Eve disobeyed and distrusted Me and exited the Garden of Eden, humans have chosen to leave Eden. Why? Know this – I have never abandoned or left you! You are My beloved child. I love you and want what is best for you. Leaving Me and putting distance between us is not what is best for you. It is like the earth deciding to leave the sun in order to go it alone!

The world is no longer a garden but a waste-land. It is not My wish that you live in a polluted environment. There is still time to turn things around. Imagine living in a filthy house! Is that a sane way to live? Is it a healthy way to live? Why, then, is man filling the world with physical, mental and emotional filth?

All the citizens of earth are spiritual refugees. They left their true Home and Homeland and there is no place on earth like the Home they left. I AM your true Home! Come home. Stop migrating from one person to another, from one pleasure to another for none of them can fully satisfy you. It's as impossible. As a bird returns to its nest, return to Me.

In Me you will find asylum. In Me you will find rest for your soul. Come home dearest, come home.

CHAPTER NINE

YOU'VE GOT EMAIL!

I never tire of receiving letters and cards from friends! I listen for the postman in the mornings and my excitement mounts when I hear the flap of my letterbox open. I rush downstairs. Ah, to see a handwritten envelope with my name on it! Handwritten envelopes are from friends or family - communication from businesses are seldom, if ever, handwritten.

What has happened to the writing of letters and cards? Writing by hand requires effort, paper and stamps have to be purchased. Thought is applied and words carefully chosen because it takes time to write a handwritten letter. Once completed, the letter is posted and its journey continues. An essential part of the writer becomes part of the letter through spiritual osmosis so when you receive it, you also receive something intangible from its author. The world is impoverished by the demise of handwritten letters, notes and cards.

Computers have transformed communication. Personal handwriting has been replaced by impersonal, electronic typeface that lacks the uniqueness of a handwritten letter. The major advantage of electronic mail is its immediacy as we can send and receive emails in sheer seconds!

We are encouraged to sign-in, log-in and do our transactions online. It's rare to walk into a business premise and talk, face-to-face, with a person. Whenever I phone a business, I am forced to listen to an electronic voice giving me a list of options and blaring music before being connected (only as a last option!) to a person. While I wait interminably, I am bombarded with advertisements! Where are the days when the customer was king/queen! The 21st century customer must do the leg-work, dialing, requesting and so forth and we are urged to be "proactive" in our business dealings and transactions! The buck now starts and stops with the client/customer.

This morning I noticed a Dutch bicycle standing outside a bicycle shop so I went in to make enquiries. The owner/assistant asked me to wait as he was conversing with a friend of his, so I complied. When he had finished his chat, I made a few enquiries and exited the shop. I studied the bike a bit more and decided to return to the owner/assistant to ask the price of the bicycle. He was busy with a customer this time. This wasn't a problem for me but, what struck me were his lackadaisical attitude and impression that I was intruding on his precious time by my enquiries! The city isn't exactly flourishing and many empty shops are to be found on almost every street in town!

Have you seen the movie You've Got Mail? The computer pinged to alert the person that he had mail. When I switch on my laptop, the first thing I do, is check my Inbox. Receiving emails is not as exciting as receiving a handwritten letter, though. I have excellent news - we daily receive email from God i.e. ethereal mail! Ethereal means: of the heavens and light and delicate.

Every day, since we were born, the Beloved has sent us email. There isn't a day He doesn't contact us to let us know that we are loved, thought of and remembered. Days and even weeks may go by without me readings my emails on the laptop but they are stored in it, awaiting my attention. They have been sent to me and the emails continue to arrive and pile up until I have time to read or delete them.

We probably all know someone who has gone away for a long spell and returned home to find the letterbox or door mat full of post. Whilst away, the mail kept arriving. When the majority of the mail consists of bills, we groan and put them to one side. They are certainly not the type of post we welcome or want. The emails God sends come from Him (Heaven) and are composed in the upper, higher regions. The author of our messages is God and they contain words of light, love and purity. The Father sends something of Himself through His messengers and messages. Heaven operates on a different level and vibration than earth does for earth's vibrations tend to be dense and heavy due to sin i.e. violence, hatred, anger, corruption, bigotry etc. How we need the freshness, delicacy and lightness of the Beloved's messages! Receiving and absorbing them lifts our vibrations and spirit!

The Israelites had to venture outdoors to collect the manna God sent them in the wilderness on route to The Promised Land. Likewise,

God sends us unfailing manna (messages) but we must collect and ingest them. It's no use complaining that God is silent if we never expect to hear from Him! The Beloved faithfully sends us manna (mail) just as He faithfully sent manna to the Israelites but we have to actively expect and gather these communications. God won't spoon-feed us! He provides for us but we must do the gathering. The manna had to be collected daily as it would be inedible the following day, so, the Israelites had little option but to gather and ingested on a daily basis. The Beloved sends us spiritual manna every day and it is our responsibility to gather and ingest this spiritual sustenance daily. There is no postponing with God! If we do postpone having a relationship with the Creator, we go spiritually hungry and weaken ourselves in consequence. We can't have a haphazard relationship with our Creator if we desire strength and courage to journey through life to our Promised Land.

The Ten Commandments were wise. Today, the commandments tend to be ignored and regarded as archaic. The Israelites tried to apply the commandments – which were a moral code of behavior, but gradually ignored and forgot them as they were having too much of good time to need or heed them. Society sank into immorality and chaos. Despite this desertion, God continued to faithfully communicate with them. He sent messages via Moses, Elijah, Samuel, Hosea, Amos, Jeremiah, Isaiah and many others. Thankfully, there have always been those who are receptive to God and his messages. It came as a startling revelation that The Beloved did not wish to communicate with a select few but desired a one-to-one relationship with everyone! Wildebeest, zebra, other wild animals and birds migrate due to genetic coding and humans are encoded with God at their deepest level!

In childhood, I used to listen to a story over the radio. It was in serial form and called, "No Place to Hide." It was gripping! There really was no place to hide as the villain's hiding place would be discovered and s/he would be flushed out! Adam and Eve also tried to hide away! How foolish for with God there is no such thing as no place to hide. It was futile for Adam and Eve to attempt hiding by using camouflage – just as it is futile for us to hide from God. Coo'ee, He knows exactly where we are! Oh, the games we humans play! People thought the heart is the seat of the soul but then Dr. Christiaan Barnard transplanted the first human heart and that destroyed that notion. The soul is not located in any organ of the body for it is intangible and immaterial. God doesn't engrave His messages on stone anymore but in our hearts and souls - the very core of being where God is encoded.

We have become God-deaf and grown tired of being told from pulpits that we are sinners, fallen, gone astray and don't have a snow ball's chance of going to Heaven! There was the outside chance of getting on the right side of God by appeasing Him and being rewarded with a free-pass to Heaven if we played by the churches rules and donated a wad of notes. Being on the right side of God was always conditional. Sometimes, we try really hard to be good and obedient but eventually we stop trying because we always fall far short of our intentions. Why be receptive to hearing from God if we have been led to believe that we are sinners, unworthy and doomed to eternal hell?

Halloween is approaching and many stores have displays of frightening attire and ghastly facial masks. It is a commercial gimmick, but, do our children need to be frightened unnecessarily? Yet, that's exactly what some churches and other religions have done to children and adults – frightened them stiff! People have been lambasted from pulpits with sermons of hell, damnation, purgatory, limbo, everlasting fire and informed that babies have to be baptized to avoid the prospect of dying "unsaved." These sermons, teachings, beliefs, doctrines and dogmas have put the fear of God into us and filled us with terror. No wonder so many have fled the church and given up on God! Trick or Treat? Obey the church and go to Heaven or disobey the church and go to hell! Other religions are equally guilty of portraying The Beloved as a monster. I have met a couple of people who are terrified of dying because they are afraid of God and fear spending eternity in hell. I recall a joke about a fiery priest who was preaching hell and damnation and who shouted to the congregation, whilst loudly thumping his fist down on the pulpit to make his point: "There will be wailing and gnashing of teeth in hell!" A shaken parishioner put up his hand and timidly said, "But, I have false teeth!" The priest retorted, "Teeth will be provided!" It makes my point crystal-clear. Not surprisingly, people have become cautious about hearing from God. At Halloween, when a child knocks on your door and you are confronted by a frightening costume and terrifying mask, you know that beneath the grotesqueness is a child. Similarly, God knows that beneath and behind all our foolish, ugly, ghoulish masks and behavior is a beautiful, precious, irreplaceable beloved child of His.

We had youthful visitors from the USA whose parents were concerned for their well-being and safety. They sent messages to us enquiring if we had met their children. We had. We made their visit as enjoyable as possible and then they left for Amsterdam. We received emails from the parents thanking us for the happy time their children had spent with us. That's what loving, caring parents do! Children are always in the thoughts and hearts of mom and dad who desire happiness, safety, success and well-being for them. This is especially so when they leave the security of family and home and venture into the big, wide, and, sometimes, wild world. It is difficult for parents to let go of their children but they know the time will come when they will have no option but to let them go. It's called the empty nest syndrome! God loves us as His dear, beloved children and He desires that we be happy, successful, joyful have well-being and are safe.

We are on a journey. We left Home when we entered into a physical body. We are in a faraway country but that doesn't mean God has forgotten or abandoned us. Just like the parents in Seattle who continued to love their children when they were far away in a foreign country; so God loves us. He is deeply interested about our life journey and keeps in constant touch with us, assuring us of His love. Our Father wants us to be happy, safe and joyful. He sent us on a journey with the request that we assist fellow sojourners, and sometimes, we encounter angels disguised as humans! God observes the way we treat folk and thanks us when we make life a little more bearable, pleasant and enjoyable for them. Let's take the time to acknowledge and thank our fellow travelers who reach out in kindness, gentleness and generosity to us.

Sin is not an offence against God but an offence against self and others. Whatever destroys peace or undermines security is sinful - it is sinful because it opposes God desire for His children. Which parent wants his child to be unhappy, fearful, insecure or sick? Certainly not a "normal" parent! How then can anyone imagine that the Holy Father wishes or wants that or less for one of His children? A parent watching his beloved child slide into addiction and who witnesses its ravages knows the hell of worry and torment. A mother watching her son speed in a car or on a high-powered motor-bike, knows anxiety and anguish. Parents sometimes suffer unimaginable heartache and heartbreak because they love their children. Unlike the detached, aloof ancient gods, God's heart is torn in anguish when one of His children gambles with his life through foolish, destructive, irresponsible behavior.

The Beloved's letters are light and delicate. They coo. They signal to us to stop ...... to listen. They are amorous messages. God knows that we are fragile dust. Teenagers and young adults think and behave as if they are immortal and invincible – their souls are but not their physical bodies. Life is much bigger than we are and will continue long after we die.

I used to get into trouble when I was young because I was strong-willed and stubborn and often put my life in danger. One day I tried to capture a wild horse to ride it. I nearly broke my neck! When my mom found out she told me that my dad would lambaste me. I didn't know what it meant but I imagined myself being roasted slowly like a spit-pig. I was terrified! My dad didn't lambaste me but, he was very, very angry. I didn't understand his anger because I didn't think my actions warranted it –I had merely wanted to capture and ride a wild horse! I misunderstood him because he wasn't angry as such but extremely upset because I had put my life in danger. I had to assure him that I would never again do something as dangerous or foolish without telling him what I planned on doing. But, as unpleasant as it was, I felt happy and relieved because my dad cared. It was preferable than him shrugging his shoulders and saying, "If she wants to be stupid; let her. It's her neck!" Many young people are out all times of the night, doing goodness knows what, without anyone caring one iota where they are, who they are with and what they are up to! Some youngsters bitterly complain when their parents give them curfews and insist on knowing where they are going and with whom they will be but they ought to get on their knees and thank God for parents who care and who love them rather than gripe and curse the curfew!

We all put our lives at risk sometimes – knowingly and unknowingly for life and living are precarious. God cares about us, what happens to us, what we are doing with our lives and about the consequences if we choose to live foolishly. We all capture and ride "wild horses" in life without a thought of the possible outcomes. The Beloved cares about the consequences of our actions. Just as my dad got upset because I did a dangerous thing that could have wrecked my life, so too does our Creator get upset with us when we do silly, foolish, reckless things without considering the repercussions. We can be real jerks! We shoot ourselves out of the cannons of life with fingers crossed and blindly trust it won't end in tragedy. We don't consider the anguish, pain and suffering our ill-considered actions will inflict on us or the worry, stress and anguish we cause those who care about and love us.

Nobody likes the word, sin. It sounds ancient and cloaked in mystery. Whether we do or don't believe in God and sin, it doesn't alter the fact that both are realities! We see sin's evidence all around us i.e. torturing of animals and humans, child pornography, rape, murder, war etc. Would we rather a remote, detached God who doesn't care one jot - or a Creator who is loving, compassionate, merciful and who cares about us and our life? When will the penny drop that God is LOVE and our Creator and that we belong to Him? We are delusional if we think we belong to ourselves and not accountable for how we live life! Our words and actions affect other people. My dad had to be firm with me in order to protect me and sometimes God has to be firm with us. God knows what is best for us and wants to protect us from unnecessary heartache and harm. The Scripture states, "Today, if you hear the voice of God, harden not your hearts." Spiritual hardening of the heart is dangerous. Who wants a hardened, calloused heart? We see evidence of this type of heart-hardness all around us. I again ask; what kind of Creator do we want? - a shrug-of-the-shoulders, "whatever you want my dear" God or One who coos in gentle, delicate, amorous tones but who is also tough and firm when needs be?

I have a friend who was a Pre-Primary teacher for many years. She never raised her voice or shouted and the children listened. When she spoke; she meant business and the children knew it. Children and young people are immune to raised voices and being shouted at. They ignore both. A raised voice and shouting no longer command attention and have lost the power to intimidate. When we try to make a point by shouting, we go unheard. People may feel empowered by raising their voices or shouting but it signifies loss of self-control and frustration. The person who is in control of him/herself doesn't need to shout and how a thing is said is more effective and more important.

The Beloved doesn't play games with us and nor does He shout. God is not frustrated or irritated. My dad was firm with me when he needed to be and that firmness was rooted in love and his concern for my well-being. Many people regard God as a jolly Father Christmas! For them, His role and purpose are to lavish gifts on us and chuckle good-heartedly at our antics. For such, God is too jolly to reprimand when we misbehave but God isn't Santa Clause! He not only coos to us but also chastens. Imagine a mother cooing to her son when he is about to drive his motor car whilst under the influence of alcohol or drugs! Her voice will most definitely not be soothing or gentle! Allow me to share with you from 1 Kings Ch. 19 about how one of God's prophets had to learn a tough lesson he would never forget. Elijah challenged the prophets of Baal under the leadership of King Ahab and his wife Jezebel to a, "Let's see whose god is the real god, shall we." contest on Mt. Carmel. The contest would prove once-and-for-all whether Jehovah or Baal was God. In a dazzling display, the water-drenched Baal alter was completely consumed by fire - the offering, alter stones and even the dust were obliterated! Flames licked up the water that was in the water-filled trenches. Wow! Elijah was on a spiritual high….. but not for long. He was overcome by fear and fled for his life into the wilderness when Jezebel threatened to kill him for the loss of her prophets and the obliteration of her Baal alters. Not only was he afraid; he sank into deep depression and wished for death. Talk about an emotional roller-coaster ride! Elijah, alas, didn't die. He reached Mt. Horeb and found a cave. God spoke to him, "What are you doing here Elijah?" Hmm, not at all what Elijah expected! God is the master question-asker and not inclined to give explanations. Elijah probably thought to himself, "You got to be kidding!" Instead, he replied, "I, even I only, am left, and they seek my life, to take it away." He really believed this for earlier, in 1 Kings 18:22, he had also said, "I, even I only, am left a prophet of the Lord; but Baal's prophets are four hundred and fifty men." The time was ripe for God to teach Elijah a lesson. He instructed Elijah to exit the cave and stand upon the mount before Him. Seems he didn't. Suddenly, there was a great, strong wind that shook the mountain and smashed rocks into pieces, but, God was not in the wind. Next - an earthquake. More rattling and shaking of the mountain ensued, but, God was not in the earthquake. Finally, (and by now Elijah must have been on the brink of a real nervous breakdown) there was the finale – fire. But, as in the other two spectacles, God was not in the fire. After all the external din and noise had subsided; Elijah exited the cave and heard a still, small voice. Not exactly what Elijah had expected - God talking in a small, still voice! Now Elijah's ears perked up. He covered his face with his mantle and listened intently.

What is meant by a still small voice? A still, small voice is a composed, controlled voice. It is a way of talking that makes you sit up and take notice for it commands attention. The voice is full of power and authority and lets you know it means business. God doesn't rant and rave or shout. Once more the Lord asked Elijah, "What are you doing here Elijah?" God doesn't mince His words. Again Elijah trotted out his lament and implied that he was indispensable to God and that the weight was too heavy to carry, "I, even I only, am left; and they seek my life to take it away." No cooing from God. He didn't say, "There, there my little brave one. Here's a sweet as reward" Instead, Elijah was told that he was not the only one left who had forsaken Him but that there are 7000 others beside him. The Beloved didn't send Elijah off to a spa for a massage and a bit of rest and relaxation but instead sent him back into the wilderness and to Damascus with a job He wanted him to execute.

You've got mail. The Beloved will tell you gently of His love and concern for you but will also use His composed, controlled, quiet and firm voice when necessary. The small, still voice flattens our inflated egos, deflates our foolishness and dashes the idea that we are indispensable. God may pose questions to us such as, "What are you doing here?", "Have you taken and eaten of the fruit I told you not to eat?" and many other such penetrating questions that strip away our masks and gets to the nitty-gritty of the matter. God may also give explicit orders, such as, "Come out of your cave of hiding and escapism and face reality!" or, as with Elijah, issue instructions to travel into a personal wilderness experience or go to our own particular Damascus. There will be occasions when He will smash our grandiose delusions just as He did to Elijah who erroneously thought that he was only one who hadn't deserted God or that he was indispensable to God. Poor Elijah thought he had worked long and hard enough and, therefore, deserved to retire in Heaven but God isn't Santa Clause! Because of His love, He sends us regular mail - some mail will assures us of His everlasting love and other communiques will caution, advise, reprimand and chide. A day consists of day and night and love consists of gentleness and firmness.

Oops - you've got mail!

Coo'ee My dear child,

When last did you talk to Me? When last did you take the time to say Thank You?

People say that I am silent and that I keep my distance but the truth is I AM always communicating and always present.

Draw aside from the tumultuous world and find peace and rest of mind and body. The world is driving people crazy. World leaders have nothing to offer. They are blind shepherds but not mute when it comes to foolish utterances. I AM the Good, True Shepherd. I know the way and the pitfalls. Don't let the misguided guide you - you will plummet over the cliffs that confronts modern man. I AM eternal. I AM the Past, Present and the Future. I see further and deeper than any human being and I AM the Way.

Remove yourself from newspapers radio, television, laptops, IPod, podcasts, webinars and blogs, and tune into Me. You give too much time and attention to the voice and opinions of man - yet you turn a deaf ear to Me! Why? My words are life-giving and wise.

You have eternal mail (email) from Me – they contain messages of life and hope. Read them. I dispatch them to you daily.

What a dry, lonely desert life is! It is a dry well. Peace and happiness are not "somewhere" over a rainbow …….. They are within you!

My dear one, don't let the Ahab's and Jezebel's of the world frighten you. They have air in their nostrils, just like you. Don't let them frighten you with their threats or let their threats cause you to sink into despair and depression. Just as I was with Elijah in the wilderness, so I AM with you. Don't hide away in caves of fear and gloom. People need you and I wish to send you to them. Don't retire form life but keep on keeping on. Continue doing My will and work. You aren't the only one in the world who is feeling disheartened and discouraged. There are millions of people who have not lost faith. Go in My peace.

CHAPTER TEN

SMS

Some people call it texting and others smsing - sms stands for Short Message Service. I prefer the term sms. It was developed for the sending and receiving of short messages. It is a handy tool for reminders, to keep in touch and a very convenient, rapid form of communication. Like every invention, it has its pros and cons.

It is common sight to see someone walking or driving whilst reading or sending messages. I witnessed a young man texting at a bus stop. The bus was late and he was still texting to and fro when the bus arrived! We are in mobile phone cocoons! We walk and even drive vehicles whilst our attention is clued to the small screen! It never ceases to amaze me how anyone can drive or walk whist texting or reading texts. I heard, this morning, that a fifteen year old girl stepped off a pavement whilst looking at her mobile phone screen, and was knocked down and killed by a truck! A soldier in England was almost abducted. He escaped severe injury when he was attacked by two knife-wielding men - he hadn't heard or noticed them because he was listening to music through ear phones. It was only when one of the men grabbed him that he realized the danger he was in!

Casualties of the short message service are the demise of letter writing and the use of correct grammar and spelling! Spelling of words has deteriorated alarmingly due to texting. Words are spelled phonetically and affection is expressed by symbols. Emotion is depicted by icons! Texts are charged by the number of words used, thus their paucity. Smses weren't intended to replace letter writing…. but they have. I seldom receive letters, notes or cards written by hand anymore.

Let's consider the writing of a hand-written letter. When I wish to write a letter I have to buy suitable paper, an envelope, a stamp, ponder over what I wish convey in the letter. I try to express myself correctly and clearly and strive to make my handwriting neat and legible. Once completed, I walk to the nearest letter box or post office and send it on its way. Much thought and effort are involved in writing a letter by hand and an ethereal "something" of the writer is transfused onto the pages. What joy to receive a handwritten envelope and how delicious to slowly read the letter. Handwritten letter conclusions are, usually, "This comes with lots and lots of love.", "God bless." and "I look forward to hearing from you." The world has lost something very precious with the cessation of handwritten letter and cards. When I was forced to leave most of my possessions when I relocated to a new country, I had to choose what to include and what to exclude. I chose to bring handwritten letters and cards from my loved ones. These are my living treasure. Now and again, I open one of those precious letters - it is as if the person who wrote it, is next to me and I feel their presence powerfully and palpably. They cared enough to write me a handwritten letter.

Does it surprise you to know that God sends and receives smses? In this instance, sms stands for Spiritual Messaging Service and Spiritual Messages Sent. God doesn't often communicate with us via lengthy communications and frequently sends brief spiritual messages. They are reminders of His love, mercy, compassion and the assurance that we are never alone.

I would like to share three of my own spiritual messages. A few years ago, I decided to walk through the dumps in Kimberley, South Africa. The "dumps" consisted of crushed Kimberlite from the nearby diamond mines. The excavated, crushed, diamond-extracted rocks were literally dumped all around Kimberley. It was a typically hot summer day when I decided to take a stroll through one of the dumps. I was in the center of this large, deserted site, when I suddenly, felt a current of alarm shoot through my body. I turned around and saw a man conceal himself behind a tree. My first impulse was to run. Then I heard a clear voice inside my head say, "Don't run. Return back along the same route you came". I was rooted to the spot. It seemed madness as it would mean that I would be parallel with the tree and the man. I knew he meant to do me grievous harm or kill me. I realized the Voice I heard was not of my own thinking; so with trembling legs and a dry mouth, I retraced my steps. My heart thumped fearfully. The path went deeper into the dumps then branched off to exit adjacent to the tree. I took the path. When I was at a safe distance, I called out to the lurking man, "I know you are there!" He emerged from behind the tree holding a large rock and gesticulated that he would hit me over my head with it! I fled. The police came and searched the dump but never found him. He had long fled.

The second experience is in connection with my brother, Raymond. As you know, he committed suicide and I was left utterly devastated. Raymond was born a 3rd April and died on a 3rd October - forty-one years and six months later. Six months after his death, I couldn't bear to face the 3rd of April – his birthday. It was a dragging, burdensome day. Towards evening, I became aware of the melodious singing of a bird. It seemed to go on interminably and it was so enchanting that I decided to go to the veranda to have a look. The bird was sitting on the garden wall. It was a magnificence of yellow and orange plumage and it continued to sing. I walked, slowly, towards it. Its little throat quivered as it sang. I stretched out my hand and almost touched it before it flew away. I was transfixed. Was it a coincidence? I knew in my heart it wasn't. It was a gift from God, assuring me that all was well with Raymond.

My third spiritual message occurred when I started noticing bird feathers. I had read that they are a sign that angels are present. This may sound far-fetched but I have become more and more aware of the scattering of feathers. These appear at unexpected times, in unexpected places and are surely sacred reminders. I choose to recognize them as such and am grateful whenever I see a small, downy, majestic or even a weather-beaten feather. I was attending a funeral in Port Elizabeth. I was a bit early and sat on a ranch-style fence in front of the church. As I sat there something in my peripheral vision caught my attention – a magnificent snow-white feather slowly and silently floating down. I picked it up and later gave it to the widow. Elijah experienced extreme hunger once and there was no food to be had. God sent bread-bearing birds to him! God does communicate with us and He uses the most amazing, remarkable and sometimes; the most unlikely means and forms to convey His message.

We send God short, brief messages too. Some prayers are lengthy and consist of petitions, thanksgiving, gratitude and confessions etc. but we often also dispatch small messages. These can be, "Help!", "I'm sorry!", "Please be with ....", "Dear Father, take away her pain!" or "Thank you!"

The apostle Paul said, "Pray without ceasing." He obviously was not implying that we should do nothing but pray - we have to work, cook, tidy, work etc. What he meant was that we should be mindful of God no matter what we are doing or wherever we are. We hear much about the importance of mindfulness today and, surely, God ought to be included in our mindfulness exercises. As a lover is always conscious of his beloved, so too should we be conscious of our Beloved. A person who loves finds the time to communicate. When we have no interest in someone, we can't be bothered communicating, and, thus, we distance ourselves. The litmus test of a relationship is communication. To tell someone that you are too busy to communicate clearly indicates the value you attach to the person and the relationship. Somehow, we always make time for what is important to us!

How important do you think you are to God? I can assure you that you are extremely important to Him. He assigns angels to walk beside you on your life journey. You are the apple of His eye. God knows everything about you. He KNOWS you. The Beloved understands. God knows when people hurt or fail you and when life becomes a heavy, unbearable burden. God is NOT our enemy! Allow me to share a few selected pieces of Scripture because they convey God's awesome love far better than I ever can.

ISAIAH 1:18

"Come now, let us reason together,
    Says the Lord;
Though your sins are like scarlet,
    they shall be as white as snow;
Though they are crimson,
    they shall become like wool."

PSALM 103:12

As far as the east is from the west,
    so far does He remove our trans-
        gressions from us.

HEBREWS 13:8

"Jesus Christ is the same yesterday and today and for ever."

JOHN 4:1-4

> "Let not your hearts be trou-
> bled; believe in God, believe
> also in Me."

ROMANS 8:37-39

No, in all things we are more
than conquerors through him who
loved us. For I am sure that neither
death, nor life, nor angels, nor principalities, nor things present, nor
things to come, nor powers,
nor height, nor depth, nor anything else in
all creation, will be able to separate us
from the love of God in Christ Jesus our Lord.

Coo'ee My dear one

How many words do you require before you are convinced that I love you – a million words? Would a trillion words suffice? I have gone beyond the use of mere words to show you how precious you are to Me. The most advanced soul, ever, came to earth to reveal Me. He performed miracles, raised the dead to life, spoke words that were full of life and wisdom and lived the human life. Despite all He did; He was betrayed, deserted, tortured and crucified! He rose from death and ascended to heaven. Man descended to the lowest level by rejecting and throwing away my Gift.

What more can I do to convince you that I care about you and love you? What will convince you? Open your heart and invite Me in. I send you so many messages. You run to your phone and computer to retrieve messages or notifications, then why, dear one, do you ignore My messages and notification? I hear your every whisper. I listen to your inner heart and voice. I know when you speak to Me.

Become alert and aware. My messages are all around you. Lift your head up from your smartphone and computer and become really smart by looking about for My signals and messages. I assure you, I have never stopped communicating with you. If only you were as interested and engrossed in Me as you are in your electronic gadgets!

CHAPTER ELEVEN

SPAM

I daily check to see if I have spam on my laptop. Spam is rude, intrusive, junk mail. It is unsolicited – in other words not wanted, sought or welcome.

I often receive pamphlets through the slot in my front door. These consist of: fast food pamphlets, estate agent flyers, requests for donations of money, clothing, shoes, etc. Sport clubs also push their newsletters through the slot! None of these were requested and only the free, local town newspaper is welcome. Many people have attached a sign that reads, "NO JUNK MAIL PLEASE!" on their front door but that doesn't deter the spam onslaught.

The most insulting form of spam is a card or envelope addressed to "The Resident". I also receive offers from mobile companies and cable networks for various data and broadband deals. Strangers knock on my front door. One stranger requested a donation for her daughter to go on a school field trip! Another gave me a flyer stating all the jobs he can do i.e. roof repairs, roof painting, gardening and every other conceivable odd-job under the sun - a jack of all trades and, more likely than not, master of none! People are fed-up with this type of intrusion, lack of respect and inconsideration.

Electronic Spam is a pain in the neck. I constantly receive advertisements on my computer. I am urged to learn to speak Hebrew, purchase coils and springs from China, buy a sliding wardrobe, learn Chinese, visit a certain hotel, shop at a particular shop, and invest money in some dubious-sounding investment in some equally dubious-sounding country! It is a waste of my precious time and I resent the impudence. I purchase a data bundle each month in order to access the internet and strangers have the audacity to advertise their products and services at my expense! I really resent this. Before I switch off my computer, I have to delete all the spam that clogs it. If I don't, I will be faced with a tsunami of spam the following day. Facebook is now allowing advertisements. My Facebook page is getting smaller and smaller as more and more advertisements appear on the page! Oh no, yet more spam! How disheartening! Even more distressing is the news that WhatsApp is to follow Facebook's example of allowing advertisements!

Television viewing isn't much better, either. I was watching a really good documentary last night but it was interrupted every 10 to 15 minutes by a constant bombardment of inane, irritating advertisements! I eventually lost interest and switched the television off. Talk about intrusive! I pay for my television license not to be bored stiff by mindless advertisements! No wonder people purchase broadband and box sets in order to enjoy uninterrupted entertainment. Advertisements have invaded cinemas too and these larger-than-life advertisements come with deafening, wrap-around sound. The radio too is riddled by advertisements. When I look out of my kitchen window, I am confronted by a bill board with these startling words, "You Look Deadly" emblazoned on it in huge print. How inappropriate considering that deadly terrorist attacks have recently taken place in France, Belgium and Germany! Mindless junk is, simply, everywhere!

There was an attempted coup in Turkey recently whilst the president was away on holiday. It failed. The biggest mistake the coup-makers made was the underestimation of the smartphone! They invaded the state television station, surrounded the parliamentary building, and, all was going according to plan – that is until the president's face was seen and his voice heard when a television reporter held up a smartphone. He urged the people to take to the streets and prevent the coup de tat from succeeding. They did take to the streets and the coup failed – thanks to a smartphone. We know the outcome. Ah, the power of technology and electronics! Although not physically in Ankara, the president used a small, palm-sized device to turn the tide of events. There are important lessons to be learned. Business men and politicians know the power of technology and how to use it for their own ends.

Bill boards are large-scale spam. As I travel by bus to town, I am confronted by huge bill boards that advertise everything under the sun. These are "in-your-face", unwanted and unsought advertisements. The posters are stripped off periodically and replaced with new ones. The inclement weather is no obstacle and they are often reduced to soaked, indistinguishable tatters! Neither have bus shelters been spared the indignity of the advertisement onslaught. It is Mission Impossible to avoid and escape spam. !

Last week, whilst watching news on television, I saw footage of the shooting of police officers in Baton Rouge, America. Three officers died. The lone killer was shot and killed. Whilst viewing the footage; my eyes were drawn to the background - every single pole and fence was plastered with advertisements!

Highways are littered with large advertisements. Gantries straddle highways and carry large advertisements. Are we not told, repeatedly, that it is dangerous to be distracted whilst driving yet we are confronted by massive advertisements ahead of us and on both sides of the highway! Companies pay hefty amounts of money to city councils for permission to advertise on highways. I am tempted to call it highway robbery!

The worst display of egotism and megalomania is the erecting of larger-than-life posters on walls by politicians, dictators and despots. They loom; massive and intimidatingly in an attempt to imprint their importance and power into the minds of the beholders. It is right and just to honor and remember true heroes and people who have enhanced and benefitted mankind through the medium of statues. I exclude these worthy ones from my complaint. Lenin, Stalin, Saddam Hussein, Gaddafi, Idi Amin and other dictators demanded that posters and statues of themselves be erected. Who can forget the toppling of Saddam Hussein's statue when his dictatorship came to an end? Has a statue been erected, anywhere in the world, to honor Mother Teresa? Truth be told, she probably would decry such an act and request that the money be donated to the poor and needy instead! There are plans to erect an enormous statue of Nelson Mandela in Nelson Mandela Bay (Port Elizabeth, South Africa). It will cost a fortune. Would Mr. Mandela wish such a statue? I doubt it. He doesn't need a statue to be remembered and would have, like Mother Teresa, asked that the money be given to the sick and needy instead. He loved children, so perhaps building an orphanage, school, hospital or clinic would be a more apt and appropriate way to honor him. No humble, sane person expects or wants an elaborate statue of him or her to be erected in order to be remembered and honored.

Rushmore Mountain was defaced by the cutting of rock to produce gigantic likenesses of past presidents. This is spam on a massive scale and is meant to instill national pride and patriotism. I recall a poem by Percy Shelley called Ozymandias. It is a sobering read. It tells of a statue that had fallen on its side. It lay there, covered in dust and buried by desert sand for thousands of years. The inscription informed passersby that this statue is of one called Ozymandias and urged them to stop and tremble at this revelation. But, who was he? Ah yes, Ozymandias was a "somebody" who desired to be feared, revered and remembered! Few seem to know who Ozymandias was! Perhaps, in his day, he was a man of power and influence who desired people to fear him and his power. Most likely, when he died, most said, "Good riddance!" and toppled the statue onto its side and let the sands of time smother it! We all want to be remembered - that is why there are tombstones. The sad fact is that, with the passing of one or two generations, the tombstone will gather moss, nobody will visit the grave and nobody will know who we were.

UNWANTED – we are forced to accept spam. It is foisted on us. It is covert and overt. Suggestion is used repetitiously. It is a type of brainwashing. It is so pervasive that most of us can't resist it. It is simply overwhelming.

UNSOUGHT – Spam is fed to our senses. It is a different matter if a thing is requested and sought but junk mail and junk advertising are neither requested nor sought. Consider how in-your-face the bill boards and gantries are! We see them whether we want to or not.

UNWELCOME – we don't want spam - it's not welcome. We don't invite it. Spam is most definitely not an invited guest. Nobody seems to hear us or take notice of our objections. It keeps on rolling in like a relentless, perpetual, callous wave. It is commercial dictatorship!

INTRUSIVE: Junk mail intrudes. It invades our minds, emotions, time and homes. Intrusion is the aim of spam. It oozes and seeps through letterboxes, into cinemas, television sets, computers, bill boards, gantries. It is everywhere!

The word solicitude/solicit; originates from the Latin word – solicitous, which means anxious. How appropriate! Spam creates anxiety because it is relentless, pervasive, crass, intrusive, brain-washing, time-wasting, inconvenient, insensitive, vulgar and extremely rude!

Coo'ee My dear one,

Do you remember, when you were a child and your mom sometimes bought you a Lucky Packet? Every day you receive a Lucky Packet from Me. It is full of love, just for you. Please open it! It is crammed with wonderful surprises and not one junk item.

Dearest, I am not intrusive or crass. I knock at the door of your heart. I will never break down the door or ram it open! I wait for your response. I give you My love and will never force it on you. It is freely given and must be freely accepted. I show Myself to you in and through beauty. Seek Me and you will find Me. I have sought you but it is up to you to be found. Do you remember playing Hide-and-Seek as a child? Do you recall how you searched until you found who you were searching for? I don't need to seek or search in order to find you for I know exactly where you are at any given moment. Are you searching for Me? Do you want Me? Am I welcome?

Be assured that I want you, have always wanted you and always will want you.

You are always welcome.

Ask and I WILL answer; Seek and I WILL be found; Knock and I WILL open My door to you. ASK!

CHAPTER TWELVE

HOORAY, THERE'S SPAM HERE!

This type of spam consists of messages from God. I call it SPIRITUAL, POWERFUL, AMAZING MESSAGES – SPAM! These are longer, more detailed than the brief Spiritual Sent Messages (smses), contain more information and aren't necessarily personal but powerful messages from God to the world in general. They are life-enhancing, life-changing and it behooves us to stop and take note. SPAM: Spiritual, Powerful, Amazing Messages.

God is creative and communicates in myriad, surprising ways. Some messages come via inspired writers, some are conveyed in song and many are expressed in and through nature. The Beloved articulates Himself through people but nature is His most startling enunciation. Prophets, writers, musicians, poets etc. are divinely inspired messengers. Most prophets, unfortunately, were killed for being God's mouthpieces. The Beloved's most articulate message is Jesus. Read His parables - they are depositories of insight and wisdom. Study Him!

Let's consider the modes God chooses to communicate through. I am in awe of nature! New York at night; pales into insignificance compared to the black, velvety night sky, peppered by the moon and millions of twinkling stars. It is becoming increasingly difficult to view the vastness of the bejeweled sky as cities ever-expand, are artificially lighted and blanketed by smog. Sunsets in Kimberley, South Africa, are spectacular and a wonder to behold!

Sunsets are awe-inspiring – or, should be. In Kimberley, due to red dust, the sky becomes a canvas on which are painted unimaginable designs, patterns and colors. Orange, white, fiery-red, burnt-orange, pale and dark blue are mingled and mixed and emerge as breath-taking masterpieces. The pace of life in Kimberley is slow and its inhabitants have time to chat, visit family and friends, and socialize and to stop and stare at its sunsets. The graceful sinking of the sun at the end of a day is nature bestowing its benediction on the glowing embers of a spent day. It's as if the Almighty is saying, "There, that's enough for one day!" then sighs with contentment. In summer, sunrises are energy-packed. It's the start of a new day and time to get up, get going and get outdoors. There are places to go, people to see, visits to be made, appointments to be kept and so forth. Ah yes, sunrise throbs with vitality, vigor and life.

Patients in hospitals lose track of time. One hour blends into the next and a week becomes a hodge-podge of days. They yearn to return to life as it was before being hospitalized. Patients miss the hustle and bustle of life, a canopy of blue, expansive sky plus the warmth of the sun. Lying on one's back staring at a white ceiling in hospital makes one appreciate nature more.

Trees, flowers, fauna and flora are special, unique proclamations. Imagine the strength of a tree that sucks up gallons water from the earth through its roots and pulls it up its trunk to reach every branch and leaf! The ingenuity of a tree is astounding! Trees absorb carbon dioxide in the day and release oxygen at night, plus, photosynthesis is mind-boggling! Truly, trees are God-masterpieces of ingenuity. They provide timber for houses, wood for furniture, fuel for fire, a roof over heads and caskets in death. Have you seen a baobab tree close-up? Have you seen its enormous flower that opens once every fifty years? Neither have I but I would very much like to see both. We owe so very much to trees and should preserve and conserve them – not hack and hew them mindlessly.

I was driving through the Great Karoo in South Africa. It is vast and, arid. In the distance, I saw a single tree growing in yellow dry grass. It was the only tree for many miles. My thoughts turned to that tree. Was it lonely? How did it survive? Why weren't there other trees? How did it take root there? Where did it come from? It rooted where it fell and adapted to the harsh, unfriendly environment and, somehow, survived and grew. We, however, are often discontent with our surroundings. We long for Brigadoon, a Shan-RI-La, Nirvana or Fairyland - a magical place where the grass is greener and where life seems sweeter, congenial and easier. Life challenges us to adapt, grow and bloom where we are. That doesn't imply that we shouldn't be ambitious or devoid of an adventurous spirit but kicking against the goads blinds us to opportunities and withers the adventurous spirit. When we have a discontented state of mind we waste our energy on daydreaming about being where we aren't, wanting more than what we have and longing to be with absent others rather than being present to those we are with.

God's natural tranquilizer is all around us in the form of the many shades of green in nature. We benefit from this calming, green balm whenever we feast our eyes on it. I saw an aerial photograph of a major European city and it revealed row upon row of buildings constructed from brick, mortar and steel! There was a paucity of handkerchief-sized parks and a mere scattering of living green. How sad and unnatural!

Jesus urged us to consider the birds and lilies - pause, look and study nature. Ah, but we are too busy. We have places to go and things to do. Who has the time to notice flowers, trees, birds and lilies? This is the modern-day lament. It's ironic that flowers adorn coffins and fill churches when burial services take place and that petals are gently dropped into the grave when we die? It will be too late then to pause, ponder and enjoy the lilies and flowers!

I was in a bus last week when my gaze was transfixed by startling beauty. Along the lane, and cascading over a wall, were hundreds of red, white and pink clusters of roses. What an Eden! Whenever I travel that route, I find myself growing in excitement as I near the wall of roses. Long ago someone planted those rose bushes and the person may be dead now but s/he left behind a legacy of beauty for others to enjoy. Tulips, roses, lilies, and thousands of different varieties of flowers of shrubs enrobe and beautify our planet. Imagine earth without its birds, lilies, flowers, trees and shrubs! I won't even attempt to. Without them, earth will become like mars i.e. wind-swept, dusty, scorching-hot and barren.

Inspired writings originate in God. I read the Bhagavad Gita – short and beautiful and I enjoyed reading it. I have read the Bible. The Bible is a library of sixty-six books comprised of 39 Old Testament and 27 New Testament books in the canonical version. Many other books should have been included; but, for some reason, weren't. Some of them can be found in Catholic Bibles. The Bible can be a difficult, confusing book to read and understand. Bear in mind that it was written over thousands of years by numerous authors. It comprises history, poetry, songs, laments, revelatory books and letters. It requires patience and persistence but both are richly rewarded.

Knowledge of God is evolving all the time. It was a startling and shocking revelation when man learned that there is but one God! It was equally disturbing for man to learn that He was not a national as they had assumed in naivety, but a universal God! Over thousands of years prophets received revelations concerning the Almighty i.e. He is holy; merciful, understanding, long-suffering, compassionate, faithful, and a seeker of hearts and not, as they assumed, a stickler for dogma and rules. They awakened to the fact that God desires happiness for His children and for them to enjoy life, that He desires a personal relationship with people, that His lives within all living things and not in temples and churches and that His laws are written within hearts and minds and not on tablets of stone …… and, so on. This knowledge was evolutionary (progressive).

I told you that I was born in and grew-up in Kimberley – the then diamond capital of South Africa and the world. When diamonds were first discovered it was on a kopje (a small hill) and men had to dig into the hard earth and sieve the Kimberlite (volcanic rocks) to separate the diamonds from the crushed, hard rocks. A sieve, bench, grease and water were used in the sorting process. The diamonds stuck onto the grease. Here are a few interesting details about the Big Hole as it became known. It is considered to be the largest hole excavated by hand (now disputed). From 1871-1914 approximately 50,000 miners dug the hole by using mere picks and shovels. It yielded 2,720 kilograms (13,600,000 carats) of diamonds. The Hole has an excavated depth of 240 meters (790ft), a surface of 42 acres and is 463 (1,519ft) wide. Today, it is no longer as deep as it was in 1941 as it has accumulated approximately 175 meters (574 ft.) of water. I can shed a few tears now as I realize that I literally had diamonds on the soles of my shoes when I frolicked in and on the dumps in my childhood!

A few lines in my High School (Kimberley Girls' High School) anthem were: "The diamonds of our city are sent across the seas but let them go we'll strive to show her maids are more than these!" And, go overseas they did. The owners of the miners became stupendously wealthy but the miners and other employees weren't paid highly. Many miners lost their lives plummeting down the mine shafts, rock bursts or from various underground accidents. My dad worked for De Beers but when he got cancer and died, my mom was left with three children, no home and a most precarious future. Yes, the diamonds of our city certainly went overseas and the proceeds of the diamond industry went into the treasuries of foreign counties.

The same method used to excavate the Big Hole must be applied to the Bible! We have to dig deep and sieve often in order to discover its hidden gems. It is a field of diamonds! Who would have thought that beneath the hard dust of Kimberley lay a pipeline of diamonds! Many think the Bible must be read and understood literally and that it is infallible. I am not included in that number. Because it is a timeless book, the Bible cannot be subjected solely to literal scrutiny. God cannot be contained between the covers of a book! The Bible IS an extraordinary, holy, inspired book but it is not infallible. Who could imagine that between its covers lays a treasure awaiting discovery! There are many awesome, wonderful gems to be gained, however, we have to dig and deftly and persistently sieve if we are to retrieve them. It is a masterpiece of human psychology, a life manual and a God-window.

There are many inspired authors i.e. Ralph Waldo Emerson, Henry Thoreau, Wordsworth, Yeats, Shakespeare and thousands upon thousands of others. Anybody who inspires beauty, awe, wonder, purity, encouragement and hope; uplifts through their writing and is just as divinely inspired as those who penned the words in the "holy" books.

God is the Master Composer and His compositions are, well, divine! He loves music and it fills Heaven. People have been and are inspired to compose wonderful music that has and is enriching the world. There are lyrics, songs and music that are not divinely inspired. Lyrics that incite people to hate, debase, belittle, abuse, kill or vulgar; are evil. They create discord, disharmony, disease, anger, hatred, violence and are divisive. They are vulgar, crude and sinister.

Nature is musical - the music of the sighing of wind through branches, rustling of leaves, tinkling of water, slapping and lapping of waves, thunder, birds singing, pitter-patter of rain are rapturous. Listen to nature's symphonies which are free of charge to everyone.

Jesus was and is a Message. The Almighty sends messengers. I don't believe the Garden of Eden story literally but this doesn't diminish the treasurers I discover in it. The Beloved conversed with Adam and Eve however that all changed when they defied Him, lied and hid and, as a consequence, had to say goodbye to Eden. They exited because they remained resolutely defiant, showed no remorse, denied personal responsibility and weren't in the least regretful and saddened by what they had done. Permitted to stay, they would have polluted Eden in their unaltered state. God gave them many opportunities but they declined them. God did not banish them from Eden – they banished themselves!

The Almighty did not abandon or forget Adam and Eve after their inglorious exit and sent messengers to them. These messengers were go-betweens. Today, priests, shamans, ministers, emirs etc. act as go-betweens between God and man! Latin was used by priests not that too long ago. It is not my intention to criticize any church or religion, but, my point is moot. Prophets were, on the whole, killed for being the bearer of God's messages. People didn't like the message so they killed the messenger. This went on in ancient times and it continues today. Then God decided to send a special messenger - Jesus. Jesus urged the people not to worship Him but only God. Jesus was different to the previous messengers for He was God's Living Message. There were no discrepancies between Him and His message. He came to deliver God's message to us. He experienced being a human being –life's up and downs, highs and lows, joys and pains. He was lonely, misunderstood, betrayed, denied, abandoned and deserted. Jesus knew human suffering. He was tortured and died an agonizing death. Oh yes, He knows what it is to be a human being and the vagaries of life. Jesus really does understand the human condition.

When the Lord was about to be baptized by John; a dove descended from heaven and a voice stated that He was God's beloved. In the Garden of Gethsemane no dove descended and there was no voice from Heaven! One would expect the Father to respond when Jesus cried out, in agony on the cross, "My God, why hast thou forsaken me?" Silence! Jesus bowed His head, and despite no divine response, committed His spirit to God and died. Oh yes, Jesus knows what it is like to be human.

When He was born angels appeared and proclaimed that His birth was one of exceeding joy and good news. It was so then, and, it still is. Jesus, the King of Kings, was born in an animal feeding trough because there was no room in Bethlehem's inns or anywhere else in Bethlehem. Imagine that! The Prince of Peace wasn't born in a palace surrounded by priceless art, luxury or nannies. Jesus comes today and still encounters closed doors and inhospitality. No matter how lowly our state or how far we have fallen, He will come in when we open our door to Him for He enters where He is welcomed.

We are sad, caustic, skeptical, unbelieving people. We laugh and chortle at the idea of the resurrection of Jesus. Why? If Jesus was born from human seed; at most, he would have become enlightened and led an exemplary life, but, Jesus was different. He had to be. Jesus was the only being who led a sinless life. He could not be born from human seed. He was pure, holy and unpolluted by sin. Mary was chosen not because she was a virgin; but because she was pure of heart. Wonder of wonders, God found a worthy human vessel to become the channel/canal through which He could send His pure Son into the world! What a risk God took! Almost every messenger He sent before Jesus, was reviled, rejected and murdered. What an Almighty risk the Beloved took sending Jesus! What extraordinary news that God never abandoned us and left us to wander aimlessly, blindly through life but sent us many who pointed the way back to Eden. They were maps who were silenced for showing us the way. God, however, refused to give up on us - even though we gave up on Him so He sent the ultimate way-shower, Jesus who proclaimed, "I AM the Way!" This is exceedingly Good news! We may marvel at our faith and trust in God but it is astounding that the Almighty has put so much faith and trust in us!

I have read theories and speculations concerning what happened to Jesus when He died. Some say he wasn't dead at all and that He "appeared" to be dead - that after having a spear thrust into His chest to make sure He was dead! Others claim He was drugged, removed from the cross, whisked away and later revived. Yet others claim He was pretending to be dead and later whisked to a secret location. Others claim Jesus died, was buried in a cave and that His remains are still in the cave/tomb and will eventually be discovered. For these, Jesus died and that was that – end of story. Finis! Why do we find it ludicrous to believe that Jesus was "different", was resurrected and ascended into heaven? Just because we think it preposterous and naive; doesn't mean it didn't happen. God is Almighty. The word, "impossible," doesn't exist in God's vocabulary! He can buck the natural system if He wants to for, after all is said and done,

He made the system! My teachers instructed me to write between the margins; but NEVER, EVER in the margins. Sometimes, just for the hell of it, I wrote in the margins. God can do whatever He chooses to do and writes in or out of the margins - whether we like it or not!

The idea/possibility/fact of the resurrection is fantastic news! So, why aren't we ecstatic? It means/proves that death isn't the end of life nor all-powerful. Isn't it thrilling to know that our loved ones who have shuffled off their mortal coils aren't dead and gone? They are Home. It is liberating to know that we will be transformed when we die. In a twinkling of an eye; what was perishable will become imperishable, what was mortal, immortal! God banished death when He resurrected Jesus. The grave lost its victory and death lost its lethal sting. There are animals that can render even the most poisonous scorpion harmless by ripping off its deadly, poison-laden tail. That's what happened when Jesus rose from the dead! People have said to me, with sad shakes of their heads, "Nobody has come back from the dead to prove there is life after death". Oh, really!

Those who inflicted willful and intentional suffering, pain and terror on others won't want to believe in a life hereafter. If there is life after death and is ipso facto, a Supreme Being, it means that they will not escape personal accountability. Every knee shall bow and every tongue shall confess.......

THE OH-ZONE!

"The ozone is dangerously depleted." so scientists say
in grave voices and with worried eyes.
We will all burn and sizzle one summer day
and crops will faint and wither when the earth fries.

Slop, slosh and slap, on go sunscreen factor 10000 and hats
before we venture into the once Garden of Paradise.
We hurry into ponds of shade; like scurrying rats
and bake brown like oven cakes as temperatures rise.

BUT, there is another zone that is also desperately depleted!
- A zone that was once jam-packed with Oh! and Wonder

but, sadly, it shrunk as the wonder of childhood retreated
and kiddies lost the thrall and thrill of lightning and thunder.
My Oh-Zone is choc-a-block with wonder and awe
For I am a fierce, fearless Awe-Hunter and Wonder-Detector!
I knocked; it yawned wide and in I walked through the magic door
and found within - the fantastical Cave of Imaginator!

He who made the Wonder-Zone is the Creator!
who delights in our exuberant yelps of "Yippee!"
For all that is AWE-FULL, WONDER-FULL, and OH-FULL - much,
much more.
Let's pause and thank our wonderful Beloved on bended knee.

Hooray, you have loads of Spam - the type you want and need. It isn't
intrusive. Unlike human spam; it awaits your invitation and will enter
when you welcome it. This is life-transforming spam!

Coo'ee My dear one,

Hello dearest.

Walt Disney knew the Oh-Zone. Even the small, daily things were miracles
to him. Be like him. You are surrounded by miracles. You see what you
want to see. Search for miracles for life is throbbing with them. Life is a
miracle!

Many are addicted to ugly, degrading pornography. Look at
WONDERgraphy instead! Why, the planet is abuzz with miracles - the
sky, stars, flowers, trees, rain, sunshine and, so very much in addition.
These are My gifts. They will amaze you because they are amazing.

"Been there, seen that!" is emblazoned on T-shirts. How sad! How can
anyone be bored when surrounded by miracles?

Wake-up! Live the true and full life I desire you to live.

CHAPTER THIRTEEN

WWW.

Www. stands for the world-wide web. Anybody using a computer is familiar with www.

Recently, I saw a very disturbing documentary about cyber theft and terrorism. Earth was depicted as a ball crisscrossed with thousands and thousands of strands. The world is encased in a web! Our world has shrunk! Hundreds of satellites orbit it daily and cameras record life on earth from space. There is no place to hide anymore!

Air craft are so fast we can travel almost anywhere in the word within hours. Closed circuit television cameras seem to be in every shop, on every major street and many home owners have cameras attached to the interior and exterior walls of their property. Our planet is smothered by the cyber web! The world-wide web has pros and cons. Privacy is no more and confidentiality can no longer be guaranteed. Hackers can and do view, read and steal corporate, governmental, bank and personal information. This is outrageous intrusion and voyeurism. Everyone can be targeted by cyber criminals. It is reported that some governments hack into other counties data banks. Cyber thieves are stealing millions of computer accounts and selling them in blocs to the highest bidder! Government, world-wide, are under attack. Need I mention WikiLeaks and the Panama leaks? Is it possible for hackers to gain access to nuclear codes and inflict total blackouts in major cities? I believe the answer is an affirmative.

There are internet bullies who besmirch the characters and names of countless people. It is abuse of the worst and most cowardly kind. Many young people have committed suicide due to the level of torment and bullying inflicted on them by faceless, nameless cowards. This type of person hides behind the anonymity of online social platforms and are dangerous psychopaths.

The world-wide web does have pros. How convenient to have information at one's fingertips! There is no limit to what can be Googled! For a relatively small price; we can tap into a treasure trove of information. It depends on man whether www. will be utilized constructively or destructively

Can the world-wide web be applied spiritually? Remember, I told you about Elijah in the wilderness and how he thought he was the only true prophet left in Israel? His ignorance was due to the fact that telephones, mobile phones and computers hadn't been invented. Keeping in touch or updated wasn't easy back in his days as news travelled slowly. We take instant communication for granted - it wasn't always so. God doesn't need a pen and paper, a telephone or a speed of light computer to communicate with us and neither did He need them to talk to Elijah! He spoke to him without the use of optic fibers, internet or satellites via His still small voice which is faster than any computer. God talks to people in their hearts and minds and is not reliant on the Tower of Cyber or its electronic gadgets.

Talking to God doesn't require a modem, broadband, internet, speakers, a satellite, smartphone or a computer. We don't need a coded password or 8- digit or more numbers to login to Him and neither does it cost a dime.

I have been struggling to login into one of my accounts. I receive a message that states my password and number are case sensitive! I know my password and number and have tried various combinations of both; but I am still locked out of my account. Thank goodness this isn't the case when communicating with God! Many people login and out from numerous accounts daily without complaint yet we complain that we don't have the time to talk to or listen to the Beloved! He is busy; yet never too busy for us. Need I say more?

ABC OF PRAYER

P – Is for PRAISE which means ADMIRATION,
APPLAUSE, COMMENDATION, RECOMMENDATION.
PRAISE from the heart.

R - Is for RAISE
> LIFT your prayers to Him and
> LEAVE the world and it's cares BEHIND
> And let your heart RISE.
> Let the world grows dim
> Let your prayers be like aroma-rich incense; curling heavenward.

I - is for INCREASE
> So PRAY and feel the worry-weight DECREASE
> And let your soul settle in EASE
> As you pour out your heart to Him.

R – Is for ELEVATION
> This is a type of BOOST -
> SOUL-LIFT.
> A SHOT-IN-THE-ARM
> That INVIGORATES, REPLENISHES, REPAIRS, RENEWS,
> REPLACES, REMOVES.

A – Is for ADMIT
> It isn't an easy thing to say: "I did it!"
> One has to DISCLOSE and DECLARE
> And CONFESS too. You have to DARE.
> And COME CLEAN.
> For GOD knows what you did and where you've been.
> NO blaming, NO hiding, NO lying.
> And, please, don't wait to confess till you're ill or dying!

A – Is for ADORE
> ADMIRE The Beloved and praise Him evermore.
> LIKE God. To LIKE is to ENJOY
> But, please remember that the Beloved isn't a toy!
> LOVE God. Have TENDERNESS for Him in your heart.
> Bear in mind that He is always the first to make a start.
> But, above all else, it means - RESPECT the BELOVED
> Who came to earth and who suffered.

Y – Is for YESTERDAY and
   GRATITUDE for yesterday's blessings that came your way
   LETTING GO of yesterday hurts and tears,
   And the crippling fears.
   ADMITTING yesterday, yesteryear, yester-everything's errors and sins
   LET YESTERDAY GO and celebrate that God's grace wins.

Y – Is also for YONDER
   REMEMBER those dear ones who are YONDER
   And let the memories make your heart grow fonder
   As you honor those who have gone HOME
   Tell them you LOVE them wherever you roam.
   THANK them for every loving thought, word and deed
   PRAY for them and ask them to PRAY for you too in your time of need.

E – Is for EVERYTHING
   Thank God for the WHOLE LOT
   The WHOLE SHEBANG
   The WHOLE ENCHILADA
   The WHOLE BALL OF WAX
   The WHOLE THING that is your life
   For life is FRAGILE AND BRIEF
   Full of JOY AND SORROW
   But, THROUGH it all,
   DESPITE it all,
   NOTHING can separate us from God
   Who never abandons or forsakes us.

R – Is for REDEEM
   This stands for BUY BACK
   And Jesus BOUGHT BACK our souls
   And made them SPOTLESS before God
   It COST Jesus - a LOT.

R - Stands for TRADE-IN
   Jesus took our old, dirty, tatty souls

And TRADED-IN His pure, spotless soul instead
So we can be clean and whole.
Yippee!!!! I am finally, utterly, truly – FREE!

R - Stands for TRANSFER
Jesus TOOK our sins
And THREW them into celestial rubbish bins
Then TRANSFERRED His STAINLESSNESS
Into our spiritual bank account that was empty.

R – Stands for CONVERT
Now, with all that SACRIFICE and LOVE
We really should RESPOND by CHANGE.
We ought to start RENOVATING our inner being
Maybe, even TRANSFORMING our lives
And ALTER our behavior
Until we are completely TRANSFIGURED,
Completely METAMORPHOSIZED
(Like a caterpillar transforming itself from a crawling earth-bound bug
into a soaring butterfly!)
Until we become less like us and more like Him

That, for me, is PRAYER and what praying and prayer are all about. Genuine prayer is heart-sent and applies to all faiths. It is an essential part of life.

There aren't visible fibers choking the earth in its stratosphere, however, the picture on television graphically illustrated the world-wide web and made a deep impression on me. As I look out the window from the room where I am typing now; I can count fifteen wires spanning across the yard. Fifteen! These consist of phone lines, electricity cables and wash lines and that's just in my span of vision! Imagine how many wires and cables crisscross the world's skies and how many more clog the subterranean! Oceans and seas have not escaped this willy-nilly scattering of manmade cables on their floors either.

There is a type of communication taking place 24hrs a day, every day that doesn't require wires or cables: spiritual communication. Everyday prayers are being said, recited or sung. Some prayers are public such as in churches, shrines, mosques and temples, but, the majority of prayers are private. Many ill or in pain; pray. Today, someone somewhere in the world will die with a prayer on his/her lips. People gripped by fear and despair look beyond mankind for guidance. Parents pray for their children. Millions upon millions daily say or sing prayers.

Every day people communicate with those dear to them and every day the Beloved communicates with us because we are dear to Him. Just as signals are sent to and from satellites so too are spiritual communication sent to God and His messages beamed back to us. We beam our prayers to the Beloved and He streams His missives back to us. Prayer is a two-way street; we converse with Almighty and He converses with us. Earth is crisscrossed with spiritual communication.

Have you seen the huge radio dishes that stand in deserts or deserted places? They resemble metallic, upturned ears. These listen for signals from outer space and never cease listening. Imagine if we have such an inner ear that is listening for signals from God!

I have a satellite dish in order to receive signals that enables me to watch satellite-beamed programs on my television set. It is attached to an exterior wall of my house. The dish is silent however it is receiving signals I can't hear! If it doesn't receive the signal; I wouldn't be able to watch my favorite programs. Even in the most impoverished country; satellite dishes can be seen anchored to exterior walls. Satellite dishes can't be placed in any willy-nilly direction but must be positioned facing north! If it isn't facing north it won't receive a distinct signal and I will confronted by blurred, indistinct images or a "Scrambled" notice.

A few weeks ago, a gentleman painted my flat roof in a reflecting, silver paint. The paint apparently reflects heat, prevents shrinkage of the fabric and keeps the interior of the house cool in summer! He inadvertently bumped into the satellite dish whilst on the roof with the resultant effect of my dish being rendered unable to receive clear signals from the satellite. A neighbor is a television and satellite dish specialist; so I asked him to come and sort out the problem. He climbed onto the roof, used a signal meter and adjusted the dish's position. Hooray, clear signals were received and transmission was restored.

Tuning-in to God is not a haphazard affair. Prayer, to qualify as prayer, must be sincere and heart-sent. Sin means to miss the mark or to separate from. We miss the mark if we think we can give the Almighty just any old prayer! God is holy and to be respected. The Beloved desires a relationship with us but not at any cost. God commanded Moses to take off his sandals as he was standing on holy ground! God isn't our buddy with whom we are over-casual. Prayer must be reverential and not belittled into a careless habit.

One of the earliest stories in the Old Testament is of two brothers – Cain and Abel. Both offered thanksgiving sacrifices to God. Cain's offering, however, was rejected due to his attitude. His heart wasn't in the offering and nor was he genuinely grateful. His worship and gift had become obligatory. He presented God not his best, but any old thing. The gift was a reflection of his surly, bad attitude. Abel loved God and was grateful for God's gifts so he carefully selected the best to present to Him. His gift was acceptable to God. Cain erroneously concluded that the Beloved was an unfair tyrant who dabbled in favoritism when his offering was rejected. In a self-righteous rage he lured Abel to a field where he carried out the premeditated murder. This is the first recorded murder in the Bible! This story provides a powerful lesson. God isn't dependent or reliant on our prayers and neither is He begging us to worship Him. The truth is that prayer and worship benefit us. It does away with the notion of entitlement. Genuine prayer and worship are acceptable but phony prayer and worship, are not.

When my satellite dish was bumped out of position it was not aligned correctly. It resulted in fuzzy, scrambled images. If we want to hear God speak to us; we have to do three things (1) FOCUS - this means we have to align our attention. We become too easily distracted! I can hear the already previously stated lament of, "But, I'm so busy! Where will I find time to pray let alone tune-in to God?" If we haven't the time to tune ourselves to God; we mustn't complain when He seems silent. We are simply not receiving His messages (2) DIRECTION - my satellite dish has to face north if I want to receive signals that will result in crystal-clear images. East, south or west – none of them will do! No, the dish has to face north! What is the direction of your life? Is it facing towards God or is it directed to the world? Let's call the world, south. Is it facing west? Let's imagine fame and fortune as being west. Is it directed eastward? Let's call

the pursuit of happiness and pleasure, east. Is your life directed at God –
THE true north? Many are directionless and hold no life-directed position
constantly. Let me use an analogy – say I want to travel to Cape Town
by car from Port Elizabeth. This will take approximately nine hours. My
problem is that I am consulting a Port Elizabeth to Durban road map!
Durban is to the north of PE and will also take about nine hours by car.
Cape Town is south of Port Elizabeth and in the opposite direction to
Durban. It doesn't make sense, does it, to use the wrong map? How could
I, realistically, think I will arrive in Cape Town by using the wrong map?
The fault is not the map but my choice of map. Selecting the correct map
to guide me from PE to Hotazel in the Northern Cape, South Africa, will
result in me arriving in Hotazel (real place in South Africa, I kid you not!)
We have to determine where we want to go to before we purchase the
correct map and consult it.

The only direction that leads to lasting peace and fulfillment is
north –God. Jesus said He is The Way (Map) that will ensure we find
God. The Beloved has not left us directionless or map-less in the wilderness
of life. (3) LISTEN: We need to tune-in to God if we don't want to travel
in mindless circles through life. When we listen we won't get scrambled
directions.

The one consistent thing about man is his inconsistency. We think one
thing this hour and another thing the next hour, have one opinion today
and another tomorrow, love so-and-so today then change to disliking, nay,
even hating him/her for no rhyme or reason! Peter, a disciple of Jesus's,
was certain and confident that he would be loyal to Him and would never,
never desert Him. It wasn't long after he uttered that oath that he denied
Him three times! We are all Peters – so confident and certain today but
not so when confronted by danger.

I am reminded of a toy I once had. I would hold the cardboard tube
to my eye, give it a twist, and a kaleidoscope of colored glass patterns
would form. Another twist and the colors and patterns would rearrange
and reassemble themselves into different shapes. Life is like that - a rapid
formation of ever-changing, shifting events. I wouldn't put my trust and
faith in a kaleidoscope toy; would you? But, we do when we place our
trust in mankind. Many people are snapping because they can't keep up
with the helter-skelter, blurred pace of modern life. We need God if we

are to remain stable and sane in an unstable, insane world. He is the only constant. Everything else is shifting, colored pieces of glass. The Beloved is coo'eeing for us to turn away from the life's baubles and turn to Him.

Politicians engage in double-talk. Sometimes I listen to what seems a coherent speech but when I distil what I heard; I find little of value. Politicians are verbose. Their speeches mostly consist of hot air. Jesus was hungry one day and noticed a nearby fig tree. He went over to pick some figs to assuage His hunger. It must have been the time of year when the tree should have been laden with figs and He fully expected to find some on the tree. Alas, the tree was devoid of figs. He didn't find even one solitary fig however He did find an abundance of leaves! This even surprised Jesus!

So much of what we hear today is a like that false fig tree. People are hungry for hope, direction, security, assurance and reassurance but what they receive are vague promises amounting to nothing. Hot air words and promises! Sift through the promises made by big-talker promise-makers and you will not find fruit but manifold, useless leaves. A million leaves can't satisfy hunger! God isn't an empty promise-maker who indulges in hot air talk. He has never told a lie and is incapable of lying. God IS Truth! The Beloved told Adam and Eve that if they ate the fruit from the prohibited tree, they would, as a consequence, die. They didn't believe Him but chose to believe Satan's lies. Satan told them exactly what they wanted to hear. He is the father of lies and will always be a liar. The word, Satan, means adversary and that is exactly what he is – the enemy. Adam and Eve died for believing his empty promises. Satan's promises are deadly. He presented Adam and Eve with a tree laden with fruit and encouraged them to pick and eat the fruit. They complied. The fruit was deliciously; but lethal! It resulted in suffering, shame, dis-grace and death. Satan's words were hypnotic. He plied them with the suggestions, became spell-bound and succumbed. Ah, the power of suggestion! It is used powerfully in advertising today. God doesn't use hypnotic words or repetitive suggestion to seduce us. The Beloved is upfront and honest in His dealings with us. He clearly and unambiguously told Adam and Eve, "You will die if you pick and eat the fruit of that tree! They ignored the generous 99% of what God gave them to enjoy and chose the forbidden 1%! We know the end result.

Have you seen the Jungle Book film? There is a scene in it when Mowgli meets the snake, Kaa. Kaa used the same method Satan did in Eden. He hissed hypnotically imploring Mowgli to trust him. Mowgli was spell-bound. Thankfully, before succumbing to Kaa's suggestions and from being crushed by his deadly coils; the spell was broken by Shere Khan's voice! Satan's hypnotic spell is broken by the God's voice! Some people lie in order to get their hands on our money, to elect them into powerful positions, or gain our affection and loyalty. Jesus said: "You will know a tree by its fruit". If the fruit is rotten and poisonous; it is best left alone. There is a saying, "Mother Knows Best" but it is God who really knows what is best for us!

Put your trust in God. He will never lie to you, or cheat you. He is utterly and completely trustworthy. Jesus said, prior to His death, that He was going ahead to prepare a place for us in Heaven, "If it were not so, I would have told you so." In modern language this means, "I am not a liar." He said: "I am the Way, The Truth and the Life" Jesus is truth personified; therefore, there is no risk in trusting Him. In whom do we put our trust? Just as Mowgli was saved from the wiles of Kaa by the timely intervention of Shere Khan – so God intervened in the history of mankind in order to liberate and save us from Satan's deadly coils. Jesus was God's voice. His resurrection broke death's powerful, constricting hold and mankind was set free. Death no longer holds us in its strangle-grip and hold. Death's coils were unwound and are now reduced powerless.

Angels are God's servants and messengers. I have read many books about people who have encountered angels. The Bible is full of accounts of angels and their interactions with humans. Both testaments are peppered with angel activity. Angels are present in our world today. We may not see them, but, that doesn't mean that they aren't present. Some churches teach that each person has a guardian angel. What a beautiful thought! We can never be alone because our angel walks with us and will accompany us Home. No one dies alone. We mustn't worship angels neither must we trivialize them. We aren't to consult angels as we would a pack of tarot cards! They must be respected but it is God who is to be worshipped and consulted. Angels are His servants and messengers - not vise-versa! Angels are indisputably active in the world today. Some angels are from other dimensions but the Beloved also uses humans to act as angels on earth.

We have all been touched by them in the guise of mother, grandfather, grandmother, friend, neighbor, acquaintance, pet or even a stranger.

When Jesus was born; angels appeared to shepherds and broadcast the good message. The angels didn't go to a priest or to a prophet - but to humble shepherds. There are times when our intelligence is a hindrance. When a grieving woman rushed to the tomb of Jesus, she encountered an angel who comforted her with the words that He was not in the tomb, but risen. When Mary was a teenager, she heard an extraordinary message from Archangel Gabriel. She neither fainted from fright nor argued with Gabriel but calmly posed questions and then consented to the request. She had been presented with an option and she chose to consent. Indeed, there must have been something special and unique about this Mary! These were ordinary people who encountered the extraordinary and the same can happen today. The shepherds were doing their daily work but then, one day, the unexpected happened. Go on - expect the unexpected!

Spiritual www is infinitely more powerful and glorious than cyber www. It's an eternal web that reaches into dimensions beyond imagination. Trust God; go about your daily business and then, one day, something extraordinary may happen to you. God may surprise you when you least expect it!

Coo'ee My dear one,

My ears are always listening for your voice. I know your voice. I want to hear what you have to say. There is so much I wish to share with you.

Keep your heart simple and open. Don't clutter it with noise and nonsense. Make room for Me. You will always have space and a place within My heart. Mary and Joseph found no room in an inn for My Son so He was born where He was welcome – in a manger! Welcome Me into your heart.

I AM your true north. I AM your trustworthy compass. Set your life by Me and you will never get lost or life-wrecked.

Dearest one, I AM The Truth. I am incapable of lying. Don't listen to anyone who promises you power, happiness and privilege. My son, Jesus, was promised power and privileges by the father of lies – Satan! He refused to listen to his suggestions to succumb. There is always a terrible price to be paid by surrendering to his lies. They are deadly lies. Adam and Eve did die when they swallowed his lies! They had to leave Eden. What an awful, self-inflicted banishment! My promises are honor-bound. The things of this world will pass away so I say to you - store treasure up where no moth, rust or thief can despoil or steal it. What does it profit a person if the price s/he has to pay for temporal pleasure and power is the soul? The price is too high! What price can one put on a soul? How strange, My child, that people will pay many millions of dollars for a Renoir, van Gogh and so forth and yet put such low value on a soul! Truly, I tell you, one soul is worth more to Me than all the combined wealth in the world. Value your soul for it is priceless.

Make Me your Alpha and Omega. Let Me guide you. Don't trust false guides and maps. I AM your guide. Don't get lost in a barren wilderness. No matter how difficult; short or long your life journey is, you can be sure of this – you will arrive Home safely and I will be waiting for you with open arms to embrace and welcome you. In My House you will find a room, ready and prepared for you – My beloved child.

CHAPTER FOURTEEN

GRACEBOOK

Facebook was designed, developed and sold for millions of dollars – or, was it billions? People who lost contact with friends found them on Facebook and reconnected. I receive many postings on Facebook and cherish hearing from family and friends. It's wonderful to see photographs of people I know and places I have visited. Facebook is a social platform that can be used constructively or destructively by its users. It can become addictive so I limit how long I stay logged in.

Grace has various meanings. The word Charis in ancient Greek means goodwill and lovingkindness. In secular Greek, Chairo means to rejoice. All the meanings are positive and beautiful. The loving-kindness referred to is applicable to acts of kindness made by a superior to an inferior, thus, undeserved kindness.

Grace is opposite to karma. Karma teaches we reap what we sow, operates on the law of cause and effect and cannot be undone or altered. We reap what we have sown. Grace is different (Thank God!). It is the only force that can alter karma and cancel its debt. Not only can it alter the record but undo and cancel it! This is astounding news that should result in relief and joy.

As the West drifted from Christianity, it became fascinated with eastern religions and embraced the teaching of karma. I have read the Bhagavad Gita and material pertaining to karma. The abandonment of Christianity is a sad fact and the institutionalized church must assume responsibility. It has lumbered at tortoise pace and fell into a stupor. As a result of the massive scale of disappointment in the Christian church and organized religion, many former Christians embraced religions and teachings that are at odds with Christianity. Grace has been a casualty of the abandonment. Grace is mentioned no less than 156 times in the New Testament and, therefore, is of central importance.

As much as we believe in karma, we also fear it! It stands to reason. We have thought, said and done things intentionally and unintentionally that we regret and shame us. As a result of this awareness, masks have become essential daily apparel. We strut, dress smartly and appear bold and confident all the while fearing that our mask may slip and somebody see the real person beneath it. With the passing of time we become adept at wearing different masks for different people and occasions. The accumulated layers of violations against self and others results in mental discomfort. We externalize it through anti-social behavior. Anti-social behavior inflicts emotional, mental and physical pain on the defenseless and vulnerable.

Women get their hair set, wear beautiful clothes, dab on expensive perfumes and wear the latest shoes and boots - yet how many pay attention to their inner state of being? Men are no exception as they too pamper the external self. We SHOULD be particular about our bodies and appearance but should we not be as meticulous regarding inner beautification and health?

Much of human behavior revolves around escapism. Life is tough and we are human. We aren't perfect or angels and all of us are capable of despicable and deplorable things when we indulge in the lower nature. The consequences are searing and joy and ease are replaced by shame. Pain, loss, suffering, regret, shame and sorrow are the fruits of the lower, darker nature.

Lady Macbeth attempted to wash the blood of murder from her hands; to no avail. It was a futile, external attempt to cleanse her soul and conscience. Pontius Pilate tried to rid himself of culpability by washing his hands. He could have released Jesus but instead chose to bend the knee to the hysterical masses. Somethings can never be remedied by external washing. If only it was that easy! Neither can we wash our hands and absolve ourselves. Inner cleaning, the undoing of wrongs and soul purification are out of our hands. Aware of the need to reverse the wrong we have inflicted and a desire to make amends, we try to atone A desire to atone (redress, compensate, recompense) is laudable, but it can't undo the past.

I have sabotaged my life many times. Being awareness of this, I gave it thought and realized that I was unconsciously punishing myself! Hurting me was self-punishment and an attempt to atone for my wrong-doings. I am not alone in this. Millions of people, daily, sabotage their lives because they subconsciously feel the need to atone. Our psyche informs us that we are deserving of punishment, so we strive to atone and try to redress our wayward past. We hurt ourselves because we instinctively know we can't fully compensate for the damage we have done. I was startled when a relative said, "God is punishing me!" when my mother died! In an unguarded moment, she exposed her train of thought. Millions believe that God is punishing them or will punish them for their wayward, errant past and is vengeful enough to inflict suffering on those closest to them. This god demands his pound of flesh and many have been taught to believe this. They are wrong! God is Love, compassionate and full of grace!

Babies are sinless but sadly, and incredibly, the church taught that unbaptized babies go to limbo or purgatory if they die! If there's no hope for babies - what hope is there for us? A baby is pure and innocent. What kind of God sends babies to purgatory or limbo? This teaching reflects how sick and wayward the church became. Its dominant and recurring theme was the fear of God. This stems from the teaching that at birth, man is a fallen, sinful creature due to the succumbing in Eden. We don't enter life fallen – the falls happen later in life when we are old enough to declare our independence from God and choose to go it alone.

We are sinners. We don't like the word, do we? Not liking it or believing in sin doesn't make it non-existent. Sin means missing the mark (target) and separation. What are we missing? Let's use archery as an analogy. The archer has a bow, arrows and a target to aim at and aims the arrow at the target. At the center of the target is the bull's eye (a dot) and is very small when compared to the rest of the target. Falling short of the glory of God implies that God isn't our target! We fire our arrows at worldly targets of wealth, fame, power, recognition and security. Thus, we fall short of God. We separate ourselves from Him when we focus our attention on the world. Worldly targets don't guarantee lasting success and don't result in peace of heart and mind. They can't. To aim your life at God will result in true and lasting peace.

What is the purpose of life? Why were we born? Where are we headed?

Amazingly, many people don't ask these questions and so drift through life like bobbing, directionless corks on water. One minute they drift this direction and the next minute another direction as they allow the currents of life to take them wherever they will. On they bob and drift desperately hoping that the tides of life will deposit them on some sunny, palm-strewn beach one day.

We were created for a purpose. We are called by God to live a full life - not an aimless life! A called person doesn't live the cork-life! They employ the waves of life to assist them to take them where they are destined to go. They are on a mission and have a compass to guide them safely through unchartered, unknown, dangerous waters. God is their Pilot and their purpose is to fulfill their appointed life mission.

God desired and willed us into being. Our birth wasn't casual, meaningless or purposeless! With God at the center, life is full, exciting and fulfilling. Is God the center of your life? When the Creator is not the center, life becomes increasingly meaningless and futile.

An archer is not born a marksman but has to practice long and put effort into training. Over time and with practice, the arrows inch closer to the center of the target. William Tell was an expert marksman and his son's life depended on it. With heart thumping, Tell aimed the crossbow at the apple atop his son's head. His aim was true and the apple toppled to the ground. Neither do we become spiritually advanced overnight. Our spiritual development requires patience and practice.

The Pharisees and Sadducees worked hard at becoming sinless. All kinds of laws were invented, observed and enforced in attempts to prevent sin. The minutiae and detail of the laws were excruciating i.e. it was sinful to rub ears or corn through hands on a Sabbath or to lift an animal out of a ditch it had fallen into! In trying to avoid and prevent sin through excessive lawmaking - they missed the mark. People resented this law-bound God and worshipping Him became burdensome and irksome. It was impossible to remember, let alone keep all the laws and the punishments for breaking them were extreme. We don't receive God's forgiveness by obeying manmade laws! The Pharisees and Sadducees became sin-spies and sin-police and were swift to condemn anyone who intentionally or unintentionally broke even one of the laws. The "Sad-you-sees" used sin magnifying glasses that zoomed in and magnified law violations and, thus, belittled God as a result! Then, Jesus arrived - Yippee! His teachings were revolutionary and He refused to be hemmed-in and defined by manmade laws. He taught that man can never earn or buy salvation and that it is impossible for man to cleanse, purify or forgive himself as he was the one who had polluted the soul and rendered it impure. Let me use an illustration: If I put red food coloring into a 5 lt. jug of clean, clear water can I separate the coloring from it? Impossible! The dye seeped into every molecule of water and stained it red. Man cannot purify his own soul for man polluted it but spiritual purification is God's specialty.

A scape-goat was man's idea. A goat was selected and a priest laid his hands on it, transferring all the sins of the people onto it. It was released into a wilderness carrying away man's sins and left to roam until it died of thirst! The innocent animal paid the price for being the surrogate sinner! The proxy sin-appeasers included doves, lambs and bulls - the sinless sin-substitutes. How could anyone think that God would request, delight in or be appeased by the suffering, torture and death of birds and animals?

Thankfully, we no longer offer animals and birds as sacrifices to God but we continue to scape-goat in overt and covert ways. We do so by blaming others for our behavior. Aren't you tired of hearing a defense attorney claim say that a murderer can't be held culpable for murder due to his upbringing or/and environment? These are referred to as mitigating factors. Why don't both sisters who grew up with alcoholic parents both become alcoholics? One sister becomes an alcoholic and blames her parents whilst the other sister decides not touch a drop of alcohol because of what she had witnessed and endured. Both were exposed to the same circumstances and environment, however, they each chose how to use their free-will. This principle applies to all human behavior. The list of scape-goats is inexhaustible - society, environment, religion, history, schools, teachers, races, governments etc. ad infinitum. Shockingly, The Beloved has been used as a scape-goat i.e. Adam blamed God for his decision to eat the forbidden fruit by stating that it was His fault for creating Eve. If God hadn't created Eve, he rebutted, he wouldn't have been tempted and succumbed so it was really His fault. So much for gratitude then! Adam used God as a mitigating factor in his crime. Everyone and everything was to blame except them. They defiantly denied responsibility. Satan hadn't force-fed them! True, they were tempted but they chose to pick and eat the fruit. They explained and excused themselves and declined God's opportunity for them to face the facts and come clean. Defiant and unrepentant, they declared their independence from God and exited the Garden of Eden.

We sacrifice symbolic doves and lambs today in attempts to appease God. Anything used, consciously or unconsciously as a surrogate for personal wrong-doing; is a sin substitute i.e. church attendance, altruistic acts, bequeathal of money and property to the church, good works, daily mass attendance, attending Bible study classes, reading the Bible etc. I am not decrying or belittling these but unless they are sincere, humble, genuine acts of gratitude to God – then, sadly, they are sin-substitutes! Churches, mosques, temples etc. are spiritual hospitals and are for the benefit of the spiritually poor and ill – not for the spiritual elite. We are all spiritually poor and ill until we accept God's grace. Jesus said He came to seek the lost sheep and to heal the spiritually sick and broken. We are not saved by being good people or by trying to be good but through our Beloved's undeserved lovingkindness.

Old Testament David had to learn this lesson the hard way. He forgot God when he became distracted and dazzled by earthly pleasures in the guise of shapely Bathsheba! Bathsheba was married to one of David's most faithful, loyal soldiers. David succumbed to temptation, slept with Bathsheba whom became pregnant as a result of their dalliance. He was faced with an embarrassing dilemma - of being unmasked and having to explain to Uriah, Bathsheba's husband and his people who looked to him for exemplary leadership. He neatly solved the conundrum by deciding on murder. David made arrangements for Uriah to be placed in the front line of battle, knowing Uriah would be killed as a result. He was killed and it was David who really murdered him. Undeterred by his dastardly deed, David married Bathsheba. "End of problem", he thought, but, little did he know his problems were about to start and that he would be unmasked as a fraudster. God wasn't fooled by secret scheming behind closed doors or the charade of innocence.

2 SAMUEL 12:1-7

And the Lord sent Nathan
to David. He came to him and said
to him, "There were two men in a certain city, the one rich and the other
very poor. The rich man had many
flocks and herds; but the poor man
had nothing but one little ewe lamb,
which he had bought. And he brought
it up, and it grew up with him and with
his children; it used to eat of his morsel,
and drink from his cup, and lie in his
bosom, and it was like a daughter to
him. Now there came a traveler to the
rich man, and he was unwilling to take
one of his own flocks or herd to prepare
for the wayfarer who had come to him,
but he took the poor man's lamb, and
prepared it for the man who had come
to him." Then David's anger was
greatly kindled against the man;
and he said to Nathan, "As the Lord lives,
the man who has done this deserves to
die; and he shall restore the lamb
fourfold, because he did this thing, and
because he had no pity."

Nathan said to David, "You are the man."

This is an example of psychology at its very best! If Nathan had
directly confronted David, David would have found excuses and reasons
why he slept with Bathsheba and denied being responsible for Uriah's
death – and that would have been that. The parable reveals the extent of
David's conniving and heinous crime committed against Uriah and was
flushed out into the open and exposed. Unwittingly, David condemned

himself in his own outburst of indignation. The mask fell when Nathan retorted, "You are that man!" The crime was especially despicable as it was committed against an unsuspecting innocent whose loyalty to David, and wife Bathsheba, were faultless. How David must have spluttered and spurted and regretted his self-righteous outburst! There was no bush to hide behind or figurative leaves to cover his naked sin as it was flushed out into the open. Thank God when He sends you a Nathan! We all need that one person who cares enough about us not to play along with our charades and shameful shenanigans and who exposes us. Without them, we would simply continue down the same path. Whistle-blowers are maligned, but, without their courage corruption and wrong-doing will continue unabated and the culprits will not be brought to book and made accountable for their criminal offences.

No amount of hand-washing will remove sin-stain. Sin is a heart and mind corruptor. David came to the realization that his sin was not only against Uriah but also against God for Uriah belonged to God. Uriah did not belong to David for him to do with as he willed. God is the Creator of life and, consequentially, all life belong to Him. Thus, we not only wrong a person - but also God. I have heard a mother say, "Hurt one of my children and you will have me to answer to and deal with!" Hurt one of the Beloved's children and you will have Him to answer to and deal with! Jesus declared that if we give a cup of cold water to a stranger; we give it to Him too. A Witness notes our behavior. Conversely, the Witness notes how others behavior impacts on us too. Nothing is unwitnessed!

I watched a television program concerning delinquent tenants. The owner of the property entrusted his/her property to persons who undertook to pay the rent and to keep it in good order. They stopped paying the rent and the owner was often met with abuse and contempt when requesting the promised payment. Eventually, after getting an eviction order from the High Court, having to expend much time and a lot of money to acquire it, the delinquent tenants were ordered to vacate the premises. The owner was confronted with a nightmare when s/he finally regained entry into the property! Filth was everywhere! The tenants despoiled the premises and vandalized it. How can anyone live in such self-created filth and chaos then have the gall to leave it behind for the owner to clean and dispose of it? It beggars belief! It is shameful, disgusting and inexcusable. When being forced from the premises, the lessees continued to hurl abuse at the owner, wailing and lamenting that they were the ones being victimized and abused! In the meantime, the owner had to pay the mortgage bond, insurance, eviction order, bailiff bill and the expense of having to clean her/his property, dispose of the junk that was left behind and re-fit the property with appliances because those on the premises were stolen or vandalized through willful destruction! Something is radically wrong with our world and the legal systems that allow a law abiding citizen to be abused in such a manner.

The point I wish to make is clear. There are many mean, small-minded, spiteful people who never acknowledge their guilt, destructive behavior or responsibilities but who plonk the blame on the owner, system, council, weather, government, race, creed, discrimination, the property owner, bank, God – whatever and whoever they can. They flatly refuse to take responsibility for themselves and their actions.

We are life-tenants. God entrusted us His gift of life; fully expecting that we will honor the trust He has placed in us and that we will use life wisely. Life does not belong to us and neither do our lives – they belong to God, the Creator. Have we become delinquent life tenants? Are our hearts and minds filthy? Are we trashing and vandalizing the life He gave us? What kind of life are we going to present to Him one day when the time comes for us to vacate the body? What will He find when He examines our life? The Creator gave us the keys to life with the trust that we would use it wisely. We aren't entitled to life. We don't own our lives because they are the "property" of God. No amount of blaming for a filth-strewn, vandalized life will exonerate us from accountability.

We know how invigorating it feels to shower. We emerge feeling fresh and clean. Sin's makes us feel unclean –and we are unless we do something about it. If we are so scrupulous about washing our bodies, brushing our teeth, shampooing our hair, washing our clothes etc. why aren't we as scrupulous about the state of our hearts and minds? The absence of inner peace is a nudge imploring us to take action. As with David, we deny inner discomfort and queasiness and endure them until we have a Nathan encounter. It is impossible to have lasting peace of mind and heart without God.

David yearned to once again know what a clean heart felt like and longed for a new and right spirit. A complete make-over was necessary! He wished to be released from his inner prison. He knew what the absence of joy felt like for sin is a joy-buster! David pleaded for the restoration of the joy of salvation – which is a right relationship with God. He acknowledged his inability to save himself. We are free when God releases us from the manacles of the lower nature. David knew that a scape goat would not suffice and that it would be futile. The only sacrifice that was acceptable was a contrite, broken heart. Passing the back, justification and blaming were not options.

The requirements haven't changed. It isn't easy to be contrite (sincerely, truly sorry) or experience brokenness of heart - but it is the only way. We ought to bow our heads in shame when we review and comprehend the extent, gravity and consequences of some of our thoughts, words and deeds. Such shame is a good shame! It is the strong pulse of conscience. A psychopath is incapable of feeling remorse, shame or guilt. The ability to experience sorrow, shame, remorse and regret are the vital signs of a healthy soul. It means the heart hasn't become calloused, hardened, desensitized and rendered incapable of feeling the deep emotions of sorrow and remorse. If a soul is to be rescued – it must experience repentance. Contrition is vital for salvation. God isn't adversely affected by our denial of our sins and stubborn refusal to repent – but, we are! No amount of compulsive, obsessive hand washing can or will remove the pollution caused by sin but God can remove the soul stains through His Grace. God not only forgives but also cleanses and purifies.

A schizophrenic sometimes has grandiose illusions that are symptoms of the illness. We too have grandiose illusions about ourselves! It's not easy to admit being a sinner who has wronged and hurt self and other people, including those closest and dearest to us. Sin doesn't have petty consequences but, in contrast, are devastating! God will not reject a contrite and broken heart for contrition signifies seriousness on our part.

God's forgiveness results in metanoia – a complete turnabout and make-over! Having turned our backs on darkness, we now walk in the Light. His forgiveness results in inner degreasing and purification. Grace restores us to our right minds. We become new creatures, old things have passed away and everything is new! A smudged, dirty page has been wiped clean and replaced by a fresh, new page – a new start!

God is full of undeserved lovingkindness. We have every reason to rejoice (be genuinely happy). The Beloved has goodwill towards us and His creation – He is for us, not against us! God is not just kind but exceedingly kind. He isn't just compassionate but exceedingly compassionate. There are antichrists but know this - God has never been anti-mankind! Our Father is worthy of our praise, worship and thanksgiving.

LAMENTATIONS 3:21-23

But this I shall call to mind,
 and therefore I have hope:
 The steadfast love of the Lord never
  ceases,
 his mercies never come to an end;
they are new every morning;
 great is thy faithfulness.

Grace is not earned, deserved, can't be demanded nor an entitlement. It is an undeserved, bestowed gift. God is not on our level. He is beyond comprehension – yet, He chooses to lavish gifts on us. Why aren't we rejoicing?

Queen Elizabeth 2nd bestows gifts on people in the form of knight-hoods; OBE's, dame-hoods etc. and these are regarded as honors. The recipients bow, kneel or curtsy before her highness. The King of Kings, His royal Highness bestows gifts on us and titles on us, such as: Forgiven, Daughter, Son, Beloved, and Beloved Child. We kneel, curtsy or bow before a human monarch so shouldn't we do likewise to the Everlasting, Supreme King?

There is a more powerful force at work than karma. Karma is a law and God supersedes all laws. Only the Beloved is able to blot out what has been written. We are not automatically forgiven! God is full of goodwill and lovingkindness but we are not entitled to His grace! Neither should we abuse it. Cain's sacrifice was rejected because he thought God was obligated to receive it. He was wrong! The Almighty is not obligated to us. David's sincere, reverential contrition was acceptable and he did not return to his old, destructive life, unlike Cain. Repentance puts an end to the notion of entitlement and must result in a revolutionary change of personality and behavior. Verbal contrition, to put it bluntly, falls far short of what God requires.

We have heard of people who have been verbally, emotionally and physically abused by someone close to them. Once the abuse starts, it signals the start of a destructive cycle. The abuser confesses his/her remorse and swears that he/she will never do it again. The abused person swallows the empty vows and promises but it isn't long before it commences again. Many excuses for the practice of abuse are given and, often, none are given. Tragically, and all too often, someone is murdered by the so-called repentant abuser. The promised change in behavior never took place and all the promises of reformed behavior never materialized. The multitude of vows and promises were broken. They were merely hot air! They are like a seed that falls onto hard and rocky soil. When a person tolerates the abuser and his/her abuse, it emboldens the abuser to continue his/her despicable behavior.

Last night I watched news on the television and saw an arrogant, burly thug, aged about thirty, emerge from court. He and a friend had broken into the home of a woman who was in her later seventies and who lived alone. They dragged her by her hair from room to room looking for and demanding the whereabouts of money and her valuables. They also tried to remove her wedding ring from her finger! The next item in the news was about a man and his wife who had kept a mentally-challenged woman locked up in a small room for many years as a sex slave! A shaken police officer stated, after he had gone to the premises, that he had never seen such a shocking and deplorable thing in his life. The world is overflowing with too many habitual abusers who time-and-again inflict pain and suffering on animals and humans. They have multiple convictions and are released, with a slap over the wrist, and resume their destructive behavior. They forget that there is a Witness.

To abuse God's grace is a disgrace! We fool others and ourselves, but we can never fool God. He knows when we are sincerely contrite and genuinely remorseful and He knows when we are faking it. Change is never easy but if the realization of our sins and their consequences isn't enough to instill a desire to change – then, what is? We dare not abuse God or His kindness and patience.

I came home one day to find my dog covered in mud. I sprayed him with water until his matted coat was clean and mud-free. He vigorously shook his body and immediately returned to the mud and proceeded to roll in it! We act in similar ways. We "mess-up" our lives and then turn to God for help. He hears us and comes to our rescue. We emerge cleansed by His forgiveness through grace but then we return to our old ways and start the whole messy, dirty process again! Much to my dismay, my dog returned to the mud and again got coated in mud. She really had no desire to give up her love for mud and rolling in it. For her it was a, "get muddy" and then "get sprayed" game. We play games with God when we think we can mess up our lives by playing in sin repeatedly and then expect Him to forgive us. This attitude makes a game of sin, remorse and contrition. How dare we play games with God? To do so is to make light of Him and His gift of grace. If we are genuinely sorry, it must reveal itself in the cessation of dysfunctional, destructive behavior. Only God can unbind what has been bound. Brokenness and contrition are the passwords that unlock the prison door of sin and sets the prisoner free. Only the Father alters and erases what has been written and done. The God of grace is our Hope.

The Gracebook is far, far superior to Facebook. It doesn't matter if your friend request has been rejected or if someone has unfriended you. The Beloved is not fickle. He is offering you His friendship. Will you accept it? Will I accept it? How can we consider unfriending God for there is no other Friend like Him? When we reject Him as Friend; we are the losers. Our Father is the best Friend anyone can ever have. Do you desire your name written in gold letters in the most important, valuable, precious book of all – The Gracebook? The Beloved's pen is poised.....

Coo'ee My dear one

I know you fear dying and that you fear Me! Why? Did you fear being born? Do you fear your mom and dad? Truly I say to you, nobody is entitled to My loving-kindness. All humans fall far short from the life I intended for them – including you! People don't earn salivation by earning brownie points or good behavior stars from Me. It just doesn't work like that. The effects and consequences of sin are devastating and soul destroying.

When humans choose to live on a lower-level; it produces bitter, poisonous fruit. My grace can't be demanded, earned or deserved. It is My gift. I bear in mind that humans are ambulating dust and that life is fragile and short. I AM compassionate. My grace isn't lucky packet grace for it cost Me greatly and dearly! My undeserved loving-kindness is a GIFT I offer to all people – including you.

My dear child, stop and think. Do you feel alarmed, ashamed and disgusted when you reflect on things you have thought, said and done? This is a good sign! Pity the person who can't feel remorse or regret! My door is OPEN. I AM inviting you to come to Me with your burdened, saddened, weary heart and life. I WILL lift your burden and restore to you a clean heart that will again know true joy.

I can/want to alter your record. I alone can erase it. When you come to Me with sincere brokenness and contrition, I promise I will forgive you and create in you a new heart and a new start in life. I want to tear up the smudged pages - Must I? Do you want to start life afresh? This is the gift I want to bestow on you.

I want to write your name in My Gracebook - shall I write it in My precious book? I await your reply.

METAMORPHASIS

A small worm went
within a silver cocoon.
Sheltered, silent
in a thready womb.
Change apace
Wings and color
Flutter, escape, flight…..
Out came something QUITE other.

CHAPTER FIFTEEN

GPS

GPS is an acronym for Global Positioning System. It consists of a constellation of 24 satellites, their ground stations and a world-wide radio navigation system.

GPS has revolutionized life. We use it in cars to direct us, step-by-step, to our desired destination. The acronym, NATSAV means navigational satellite and all it requires is an address to guide us to the required destination. There is no longer any excuse for getting lost. GPS is also employed in the tagging of prisoners and suspected terrorists. A bracelet is attached to either the wrist or ankle and the person's movements are monitored. Unfortunately, as we recently saw in France when a Catholic priest was killed by ISIS terrorists, it doesn't prevent the person from committing murder as the tag only determines the geographical position of the person, not the premises. The global position system can be used wisely or unwisely; constructively or destructively.

Radio messages are beamed to a satellite, which in turn, beams information to the radio stations on earth. These transmissions are almost instantaneous. Not only are signals beamed to and fro but GPS make it possible to photograph almost every location on earth from space. Detailed photographs result in the construction of precise and accurate maps. Our planet has lost its mystery and charm by being filmed and mapped in minute detail and has been reduced to one big, public place.

There is another system that is much more ancient and exceedingly more sophisticated than GPS! It has many features but I will focus on only a few. It is God's Positioning System. The Almighty is the creator of galaxies, black matter, universes, suns, planets and billions upon billions of stars – in fact all that is visible and invisible. Because He created everything - everything belongs to Him!

I recently watched two wonderful documentaries on television. One was about the Hubble telescope. At first, due to a flawed mirror, it reflected fuzzy, indistinct pictures. Astronauts fixed the problem and when photos were transmitted from Hubble to ground station; they revealed distinct, clear and marvelous images of unimaginable wonder and beauty! Hubble proved that space is expanding, not contracting as people thought, and that there is infinitely far more in and to space than ever imagined.

The other documentary concerned mathematics. Someone wrote a book suggesting that God is the ultimate mathematician! Did man create mathematics or did a Mathematician make man? What is becoming clear is the order and design in creation. The atom is an ordered, intricately designed wonder. It basically comprises a proton, neutron and an electron but there is much more to the atom than these. Pause for a minute. Do we honestly believe that the design and order we see in everything, is a fluke of nature? Do we honestly believe that an organic soup is responsible for life on earth? Just who or what created the primeval, organic soup that some scientists believe was the spark-plug responsible for started the creation engine moving? It's like dropping a glass from a height and expecting all the scattered, fragmented pieces to miraculously assemble themselves into a coherent whole! If we stop outside a mansion and somebody informs us that it simply materialized, we would laugh uproariously and wonder at the mental state of the person who made the statement. It would be just too ludicrous to seriously consider. We know that a draughtsman or architect had to envision, plan and design it before it could be constructed. A builder, if he has any sense, will be guided by the blueprint. We often hear of buildings that collapse because there was no blueprint to start with! Why then do we scoff at the notion of a Supreme Designer and Builder? Scientists know black matter is a reality even though they can't see it and neither do they know what it is - yet it comprises 80% of space! Our instincts tell us that there is – nay, has to be a Creator. He is as real as black matter is real!

God placed the stars, planets and suns in space and created trees, shrubs, grasses, flowers, fruit, animals, oceans, rivers and all living things. He is the Creator of everything! According to Genesis light, darkness, plants, grasses, birds and animals preceded the creation of humans! We are positioned in time and space, born at a certain time and at a particular place. We chart our way through life and encounter different people at different times on our life journey. Many relocate far from their place of birth and others never leave the town/city in which they were born.

Our place of birth has a magnetic pull. Remembering it and reliving childhood memories fills us with nostalgia and homesickness. A relative bred and trained pigeons. He would convey the pigeons hundreds of miles away from home and release them. They flew home after circling a bit in order to get their bearing. Humans are like those homing pigeons. No matter how far away we have roamed from Home, we are all returning Home. Our Home has a magnetic pull on us.

Generations come and go and our generation will pass away. There is a pattern to life. Let's consider a few questions: Why were we born where we were? Why were we born on a particular day and in a particular year? Why do we encounter certain people and not the billions of other people who inhabit the world? Why were we born into a specific family? Why are some people our friends whilst others remain acquaintances? The answer, I believe, is God's Positioning System! Imagine if everyone was born in the same town or country or met all the same people? There is a plan and design that we are not conscious of. Why are some stars supernova stars and others white dwarf stars? Why is our medium-sized sun positioned where it is? Yes, a mind-boggling plan is in operation. The misuse of free-will acts as a spanner in the works and interferes with the Almighty's plan. We oppose and attempt to sabotage the Divine plan. This is exactly what Satan is trying to do. Remember Adam and Eve? Instead of co-operating with God; they defied Him, and in consequence lost the plot, plan and the Garden of Eden! They thwarted the divine blueprint and plan. God had positioned them in a Garden of plenty and His design was for them to live in harmony with Him and nature and have eternal life. Their defiance and rejection of His plan resulted in self-exile, barrenness, aridity, suffering and death - the antithesis of God's design for them. Whenever we rebel against or reject God's plan and design for us we find ourselves in a self-imposed wasteland that results in a directionless and purposeless life. This is not what the Beloved planned for us and certainly not what He created us for! Life can't be improved by rejecting God.

Our Father sends angels that we encounter unknowingly. Sometimes, they are spiritual beings and sometimes they assume human guises. One of my favorite angel stories is when an angel appeared to Balaam and his ass in the Old Testament. The irony is that the ass saw and reacted to the angel long before the prophet did! It took Balaam a while before he grasped the situation. Animals do have souls! I think animals are more aware of the spiritual realm than humans. How arrogant of us to think that only humans have souls! We can and do learn invaluable lessons from the vegetable and animal kingdoms. It is equally arrogant to think that we are of sole interest and importance to the Creator. We are deluded in thinking we are superior to the rest of creation. God never intended nor commanded us to dominate creation! We were given the task and responsibility of caring for it as a keen gardener would his own garden. We were to be its guardian. Jesus was not only sent to mankind but the whole of creation!

JOHN 3:16

"For God SO loved THE WORLD that He gave ...."

Humans are capable of unimaginable acts of cruelty and it is perverse to say that a person acted as an animal when he/she behaved cruelly and brutally! Animals can be, and, often are, more compassionate and loyal than humans. After Raymond died, I was distraught. I sat on a step outside my house one morning and sobbed. Gypsy, my Rottweiler, tip-toed towards me and gently put her large head onto my lap. She sighed deeply and looked up at me with eyes full of love and tenderness. I knew she understood what I was feeling and going through.

Another amazing angel story is to be found in the Book of Tobit. You can find it in the apocryphal in a Catholic Bible. It is a truly amazing story of an angel's journey to earth in response to the prayers of two people, namely Judith and Tobit. I encourage you to read it. Please note that Tobit's faithful dog is mentioned! It is a story consisting of many twists and turns and well-worth the read.

Archangel Gabriel appeared to Mary requesting her co-operation in God's plan. She didn't faint at the sight of Gabriel and conversed with him! From this account, one can deduce that it was natural for Mary to have conversations with the Almighty and His angels. For her, conversing with angels was not fear-laced and encountering them was a matter-of-fact thing. Joseph, on the other hand, had his angel encounter in a dream Ah well - God sends His messengers in whichever way makes them discernable to us.

Angels were an integral part of Jesus's life. From birth to death He was in contact with them and them with Him. It is human to question why they weren't present whilst Jesus hung in agony on the cross. It would, however, be erroneous to think that they were not present because they weren't visible to human eyes. In the Old Testament, there is an account of armies of angels standing between an invading army and the little village of Dothan. A young man was terrified by the sight of the enemy army and death seemed imminent and inevitable. The prophet prayed that the lad's eyes be opened and he beheld what his human eyes could not – thousands of angels!

Angels aren't Teflon coating against life. They are God's messengers and servants. Our Almighty never promised that He would protect us from danger but promised that He would be with us wherever we are and whatever befalls us. God was present when Jesus was on the cross. He was present in the tomb and when Jesus was resurrected. Wherever we are, whatever we are going through – be assured that God is with us. NOTHING can separate us from Him or His love!

We each have an angel who accompanies us through life and who will accompany us Home when we die. My mom was born on the 3rd of August and died at the age of 58 in 1986. It was the 3rd of August 2016 and I was busy making my bed when I paused to think of her and thank her for all she had done for me. My eyes came to rest on the clock - 11:11! In a flash of insight, I knew my mom had heard me. Call it foolish coincidence if you will but I believe God encounters and encourages us in many surprising ways.

There is a story I wish to share regarding God's use of humans as angels. It is found in Acts Ch.8. An Ethiopian eunuch was on a journey between Jerusalem and Gaza and he was reading the book of Isaiah. He was puzzled by what he was reading and wished to understand. He desired insight. The eunuch made the journey to Jerusalem to worship God. The Beloved knew his thoughts and sent an angel to Philip (one of Jesus's disciples) with these concise instructions:

"Go south to the road-the desert road-that goes down from Jerusalem to Gaza".

The directions and instructions were clear. Off Philip went as instructed and didn't know to whom he was being sent. The next part of the message came:

"Go to that chariot and stay near it."

As Philip ran up to the chariot, he heard a man reading from the book of Isaiah. It was the Ethiopian eunuch – a very important official who was in charge of the treasury of Queen Candace, queen of Ethiopia. He was a powerful man but one who sought spiritual understanding. Philip sat beside him and explained that what he was reading was a prophecy concerning Jesus and that the prophecy had come to fruition. The Ethiopian listened, comprehended and had an epiphany! They came to some water and the man asked his entourage to stop so he could be baptized. His entourage was amazed! The eunuch never saw Philip again and went on his way, rejoicing. The angel whisked Philip away and he suddenly appeared at Azotus. This was teleportation long before the Star Wars movies were made. "Beam me up Scotty."! It doesn't matter if we are Ethiopians, Syrians, Americans, Brazilians, British, Slovakians or Eskimos etc. – God knows our thoughts and hearts. He is able to dispatch angels to us wherever we are. Time and space are immaterial to the Almighty. God sent two messengers to the eunuch– a spirit angel and the other was human, Philip. The Almighty sometimes selects a human to act as angel. Can you think of times and instances when you encountered angels? Human or spiritual, they were surely sent by God.

The Divine's global positioning system is 100% accurate and the co-ordinates are perfect. Take for example the day women went to Jesus's tomb and found the huge stone rolled away! They entered, trembling, and found it empty! They stood in the midst of the tomb and tried to figure out what could have happened to Jesus's body. Was it stolen? Did somebody remove and bury it somewhere else? Who could have rolled away the large, heavy stone? Why would anybody want to move His body? Suddenly, in the center of the tomb, two men in gleaming apparel (angels) appeared. The women probably were near to fainting from shock, but, they bowed down until their faces touched the ground. The angels spoke:

"Why do you look for the living among the dead? He is not here; he has risen!"

They hurried from the tomb and went to the Eleven (disciples) and excitedly told them what had happened, however, the disciples did not believe them and thought they it were delusional and that the story was nonsense and a fairytale. The Beloved sent two angels to bring hope and joy to heavy, saddened hearts in a tomb - the exact locality of loss and unbearable heartache. The angels messages were life-altering ones of indescribable joy, "He is not here; he has risen!" Our loved ones are not in a grave, a tomb or an urn but alive and risen to new life. Glory to God!

Jesus appeared to Mary Magdala in her darkest hour. She was bereft at the tomb and sobbed bitterly. Two angels appeared to her and asked her a question:

"Woman, why are you crying?"

What an unexpected question! Her friend and Lord had died a cruel death upon a cross and had been buried. How could they ask her why she was weeping? She replied, through tears, that someone had stolen the body of Jesus and that she was heartbroken as she didn't know where the body was. For her, it was double grief and sorrow. She didn't realize that Jesus was standing behind her! With wet, misty eyes she turned around and saw someone. Jesus said to her:

"Woman, why are you crying? Who is it you are looking for?"

She proceeded to ask where he had taken Jesus's body so she could go and retrieve it. Jesus replied:

"Mary."

In that instant, she recognized that voice and who it was who was speaking to her. Her tears of sorrow turned into tears of joy! Jesus then said:

"Do not cling to me".

He was alive!

Never has there been a more important question put to any person than this,

"Who is it you are looking for?"

Indeed – who is it we are looking for?

Fear not, God hasn't tagged you in order to treat you as a fallen sinner whose every step must be monitored and registered. He watches over us because He loves us. God cares about us and our life.

Jesus's hands and feet were pierced and scarred by nails. His chest was pierced and is body was lacerated by whips. His head was punctured by a crown of thorns pushed down on it. Today, many people have tattoos engraved into their flesh. Will it startle you to know that God has carved your name onto the palms of His hands? It is a graphic, figurative image of His deep and intimate love for us.

"Can a mother forget the baby at her breast and have no compassion on the child she has borne? Though she forget, I will not forget you! See I have carved you on the palms on my hands: your walls are ever before me." ISAIAH 49:15

GPS is also an acronym for God's Promises Supreme. We should never make a promise we can't or don't intend to honor for to do so is cruel as it creates expectations, that when unfilled, causes crushing disappointment and mistrust.

I remember witnessing a scene, many years ago, that I will never forget. I used to visit a children's foster home in Kimberley. Some of the children came from broken homes, some from homes where they could no longer be cared for and other children were orphans. One day I went to the home and, at a gate in the enclosed garden, sat a little girl on a suitcase. I made enquiries and was told that her birth mother had phoned and made arrangements to collect her at a stated time so she could take her home for the weekend. The staff readied the child and told her to pack a case of clothing as her mother was coming to fetch her. The child was beside herself with excitement. She could not contain her excitement and asked if she could wait for her mom in the garden. They gave her permission and kept an eye on her to make sure she was safe. The agreed time for collection arrived and the little girl was more than ready. The minutes ticked by. The minutes became an hour and then two hours until it was apparent that the mother was not coming for her little girl. The staff was dismayed and made frantic phone calls but received no reply from the mother. The child stubbornly refused to relinquish her post and kept saying, "My mommy will come. She promised she will come! Just watch and you will see – my mom will come. She gave me her word!" But, mom never came and I will never forget that crest-fallen, sobbing child clutching her suitcase as she was gently ushered back indoors by the distressed staff. I wonder if that child can or will ever trust anyone, ever again. This true account describes the devastation a broken promise can inflict. It is a wound that cuts to the marrow and, often, the wound never heals. Let your word be your honor. Mean what you say – if you mean Yes then say it. If you mean No then say "No".

God isn't an idle promise maker. He honors His promises for His word is His honor and they are inseparable. The Beloved is utterly trustworthy. We have been disappointed by failed promises but our Father will never disappoint or fail us. I share but a smidgen of His promises here. I consulted The Revised Standard Version of the Bible.

DEUTERONOMY 31:8

"It is the Lord
who goes before you; He will be with
you, he will not fail you or forsake you;
do not fear or be dismayed".

JOSHUA 1:9

"Have I not commanded you?
Be strong and of good courage; be not frightened, neither
be dismayed: for the Lord your
God is with you wherever you go."

JOHN 14:27

Peace I leave you;
My peace I give to you; not as the world gives do I give you.
Let not your hearts be troubled, neither let them be afraid.

You can even Google God's promises on the internet! I did and there are many helpful sites. There are many more promises to be delved in the Bible and I urge you to grab your spade and start digging and I promise you will find spiritual diamonds awaiting you.

The third aspect of God's GPS is God's Power Sharing. He is immortal, omniscient, omnipresent and, omnipotent – yet, isn't it astounding, He invites us to co-create with Him? People are born without sight, without hearing, others with malformed limbs and some are paralyzed BUT nobody is born without potential or without gifts.

We have heard about people who are disabled/handicapped and who have accomplished astounding things. Helen Keller comes to mind. I used to buy Christmas cards in South Africa that were painted by armless people who used their toes to paint! The paintings were breathtaking! There are many who have all their limbs, sight and hearing etc. but who fritter away their potential and talents. Whatever potential they were gifted with, withered away through the lack of effort and drive. The potential and talents become flabby, soft and shriveled. Low muscle tone indicates an under-used muscle and low potential use indicates under-use of potential! The under-use results in weakness and degeneration. These are the truly disabled and the tragedy is that they have disabled themselves! Many physically handicapped people have turned their disability into His-abilities and their handicaps into handy-caps that have in-powered them to do and live extraordinary lives.

Jesus taught a parable. He said that some people were given ten talents (a talent was more than fifteen year's wages of a laborer), others five talents and some one. God wasn't being unfair and arbitrary in dishing out the talents as they were His to dispense with as He chose to. The crucial points in the parable are (1) God was the giver of potential and talent (2) that not one person went empty-handed (3) God expected the person to use what he had received and to multiply it through use (4) comparison belittled the gift (5) by (not using) the gift was to disrespect and impoverish it by the lack of investment (6) we are accountable to God for how we use or fail to use His gifts. Of crucial importance was how each person used the allotted talents. The worst outcome was to belittle the gift through shame, embarrassment, jealously, envy, anger, fear and then to dispose of it by burying it (non-use).

Some people are very talented. We often see child progenies and wish we could be like them. The questions we should be asking are, "What are my talents?", "How can I multiply them?", "How can I use them for the furtherance and benefit of all? "Have I buried my gift?"

I knew someone who was extremely intelligent. He never completed his studies at university as he considered himself more intelligent than his lecturers, so he dropped out of university. Was that smart? He never did graduate and wound-up working for someone who did obtain his degree. There are many intelligent people who under-use their potential and drift through life; too smart for their own good. A good friend of mine recently retired after forty plus years of working for the same company. He plodded every day and gave of his best. He will now retire on a generous pension and benefits and I wish him a long, happy and healthy retirement. Oh, did I mention that he never went to university? He worked himself up through the ranks via perseverance and hard work. Single-mindedness and perseverance are true indicators of attaining success - not the idea of entitlement due to above-average intelligence.

God shares His power with us and empowers us to accomplish beautiful things with and through our lives. To help, encourage and lift the fallen and broken is to enter into partnership with God. It is no use complaining bitterly that He should save the world whilst we stand back idly, like spectators with folded arms! We MUST use the talents and potential God gave us for we ARE His hands and feet on earth!

Coo'ee

Hello My dear one,

You can trust Me. Satan promised Adam and Eve they would become like Me, know the difference between good from evil and would not die if they obeyed him and complied with his suggestions. He lied! I AM incapable of lying! I AM truth.

Dear one, I have given you talents and gifts - use and multiply them. They are not only for your benefit but also for the betterment and enrichment of My people. Don't bury what I gave you. Think of how you have benefitted from those who have used their talents. Don't throw away the gift! Use My gift. Enrich and beautify the world. The Red Sea never parted until Moses co-operated with Me.

You can never be lost. I know where you are every second of every day. I promise you that should you run away from Me, I will find you and I will keep searching until I do!

I will never leave or forsake you – that's a promise. Do you believe Me?

CHAPTER SIXTEEN

BREAKING NEWS

When I switch on my television set to watch international news, I often see, "BREAKING NEWS". This can only mean one thing – something extremely important has taken place and my immediate inclination to find out more!

Today's breaking news was that an earthquake had struck Italy, again. Recent breaking news was the FBI reopening its investigation into Hillary Clinton's alleged use of her private computer email address whilst she was Secretary of State! Almost every day has Breaking News!

In the ancient past there was a lot of spiritual breaking news. Old Testament prophets frequently had startling revelations pertaining to God. Hosea announced deeper insight into the immensity and unfathomable love of God. Jonah, the Reluctant Prophet, went to Nineveh with breaking news concerning their wayward behavior and the future catastrophic consequences if they didn't heed the message. Abraham obeyed when God broke the news to him that he was to leave his country and go to a foreign country. Lot and Mrs. Lot listened to the breaking news about the imminent destruction of Sodom and Gomorrah and fled to the hills. Sadly, Mrs. Lot chose not to comply with all the instructions, looked backwards, and, turned into a pillar of salt! The Beloved sent Moses to the Pharaoh of Egypt with startling breaking news: "Let My people go!" Pharaoh alternated between complying and refusing with dire consequences. He lost everything by not taking the breaking news seriously. It pays to listen to important breaking news!

The New Testament is wall-to-wall with breaking news. Here is an example as found in Luke 1:26-38 pertaining to Archangel Gabriel's trip to a dusty, little village called Nazareth where he broke this news to Mary:

"Hail, O favored one, the Lord is with you!"

She was perplexed that an angel should visit her with such a message. Gabriel addressed her again:

"Don't be afraid, Mary, for you have found favor with God. And behold, you will conceive in your womb and bear a son, and you shall call his name Jesus."

Discussions ensued.

Eventually, not fully comprehending the immensity of the message, she replied:

"Behold, I am the handmaiden of the Lord; let it be to me according to your word." And, he angel departed from her. And, it came to pass."

It's not surprising that Mary was chosen by The Beloved. She trusted Archangel Gabriel's breaking news! The request didn't sound rational, logical or possible but she had utter faith in God. Please note that Gabriel went to a specific place and spoke to a specific person. Mary became the conduit through whom the Beloved chose to send His Living Word (Message) to the world.

Television networks are owned by various companies and certain individuals who broadcast news hourly, daily, seven days a week. News is looped hourly and its content is predominantly negative, disturbing, shocking, stress-inducing and alarming. No matter how upbeat I am, I end up deflated after watching or listening to the news! The effects are disheartening, fatiguing and draining as the content tends to focus on: drug lords swamping countries with their deadly merchandise, murder, child molestation, corruption, theft, nepotism, theft, animal cruelty ad infinitum. Grey-haired, grandfatherly men in positions of trust pilfer money, priests abuse children, silk-tongued politicians make grandiose promises before an election but seldom deliver once elected, parents who physically abuse their children, dictators who enrich themselves and their cronies by using a country's national purse as their own, bombed-out cities with flattened buildings, soldiers strapped with bullet belts and vests, heavy artillery and guns, tribal war, faction wars, religions wars, suicide bombers, lunatics driving huge trucks who deliberately mow down pedestrians ....etc. - the list of pictorial/audio images is relentless, graphic and exhausting! How I YEARN for good news. I am sick and tired of sensationalized breaking news that depicts acts of mindless destruction, man created famines and mankind at its worst. Is it any wonder that people are losing hope, faith in God and their minds!

Politicians are incapable of delivering what the world is most in need of – hope! Churches and world-wide religions have not been of much help either – rather than being vehicles of healing and stability; they have added to the levels of confusion, despair and conflict. People are desperate and despairing and entire societies are at snapping-point. The world is frantically looking for a savior and this fraught desperation is dangerous. ANYONE who appears to have solutions for mankind's problems will attract followers who will view him/her as a global savior. We are sheep without a shepherd. Yet, despite the critical state of the world the UN, NATO, EU and world leaders still refuse to turn to God! People have listened to and believed past dictators who brutalized and impoverished them and today people are listening to and believing dictators who are brutalizing and impoverishing them! What will it take for mankind to turn to the Beloved and listen to Him? Mankind ignores God and seems hell-bent on self-destruction and the destruction of our glorious planet. This is sheer madness!

The time to turn to God is NOW and this Breaking News urgently needs to be broadcast and looped hourly around the world. Take a look at what we are doing to each other and our planet! The Almighty God is the Creator. We don't belong to a political party, a politician, priest, shaman, emir, church, mosque, temple – we BELONG to God! We have forgotten this fact. We are SO focused on the external, material, consumer-driven world; that we are blind to the fact that we have souls! Breaking News – there is NO human savior! No one knows how to save the planet for mankind seems determined to destroy it. For crying out aloud - politicians are still arguing and dallying about carbon emissions, use of fossil fuels, hacking down of forests and can't reach consensus; let alone binding lasting agreements that will enforce quick and drastic change! While they loiter with reaching consensual agreement and set yet another date for a future meeting to discuss global warming and climate change, they blithely ignore the fact the planet can't wait until it suits them to convene! I recently saw footage of oil-soaked skies in Mosul, Iraq, that literally blocked out the sun and also footage of a Russian war ship in the English Channel, spewing out huge plumes of thick black smoke from its stacks ! Our planet is being raped, plundered and relentlessly assaulted. Who can forget the cavalier (high-handed, arrogant, carless, casual, haughty) manner in which atomic and hydrogen bombs were detonated in deserts, on islands, in oceans and seas and deep under-ground! Earth cannot and will not tolerate this abuse any longer. God is the Creator but man has become its Violator! Some job we have done in our entrusted role as earth's gardener!

We DARE NOT repeat the same mistake people made prior to the Flood! Many, most likely, scoffed and laughed when Noah told them that he was building an Ark in order to escape the approaching flood. They would not/could not accept his warning/prophecy for theirs was the "business as usual" attitude. They didn't laugh long. BREAKING NEWS – We can't and dare not continue with our" business as usual" attitude either. We simply cannot afford to continue behaving as we are because we are in a state of global emergency! A "flood" is coming and its repercussions will be beyond imagination. I don't know what form the catastrophe will take but it will affect life forever on the entire planet. I recall watching the devastation caused by the tsunami in Thailand and Malaysia on Boxing Day 2004. The waves pulverized much of Phuket. Boxing Day 2004 was most certainly not business as usual and thousands upon thousands of people lost their lives, property and belongings. I will never forget that breaking news or the images!

God offered mankind an escape route prior to the Flood but the majority chose not to listen. Noah and his family used the available grace time to construct a boat and they didn't stop building it until it was complete. Mankind is in grace-time but nothing substantial and suitable has been devised to survive what is coming. The hands of the clock are irreversibly and irretrievably ticking away the opportunities grace is affording us. Jaw-jawing will no longer suffice. We are in Grace-time! When catastrophes strike; God is too easily blamed. Natural events occur i.e. earthquakes etc. and these are termed by insurers as Acts Of God! Why is God blamed for catastrophic events yet not given the credit for life-sustaining order? Typical of mankind to blame God for all that is negative and destructive! Destructive calamities are not God's will or punishment. The Beloved loves us. He is merciful. His warnings of possible devastations if we don't change course comes as urgent wake-up calls that can avert tragedy. Now is the time. We must not tarry! We punish ourselves – not

God! We are destroying ourselves – not God! No politician, government and no super power has the answer or solutions. It is time for mankind to humbly return to its Creator for He alone is the Answer and Solution! Our planet is billions of years old but it has never before faced such levels of degradation and abuse as in modern times. It is sheer, utter, inexplicable madness to do what we are doing to our planet.

HICKORY DICKORY DOCK

Oh Hickory, Dickory Dock
We're all in for a nasty shock!
atomic bombs here and there.
My God, how we will see the smoke and the flare!
Oh yes, we're all in for a nasty Hickory, Dickory shock!

Explosions in the desert and in the sky -
And if we don't wake up soon, we're all going to die!
One island, two islands obliterated in the sea
and the world wrings its hands and laments, "O, woe is me!"
Oh Hickory, Dickory Dock what a nasty shock.

Why can't we live in peace and harmony?
Why this insatiable greed and lust for money?
God gave us a magnificent flowery Paradise
but it's up to us if it lives or withers and dies.
Oh Hickory, Dickory Dock
It's time to stop the damned, mad nuclear clock!

It is a minority who are making life on earth intolerable. Throughout history we have elected some leaders who, frankly, showed signs of mental instability. We have been groomed to be passive and indecisive and, as a result, have eagerly and happily looked to "powerful" others to think, decide, act in our "best" interests and take care of us. Some of these so-called saviors: detonated atomic bombs, exposed people to sarin (nerve gas resulting in asphyxiation) – including children, dropped deadly chemicals on opposing sects, rained-down chemicals to defoliate trees and vegetation, napalm-bombed villages, released mustard gas on enemies, beheaded people and used terror against civilians in order to make a point or a statement! Power is intoxicating to the ego-driven narcissist. Doubtlessly, there have been, and are, good-intentioned, hard-working, ethical and honest politicians who had and do have integrity BUT how many wise, humble, exemplary world leaders have there been in recent history and how many are there today?

We must snap out of our self-induced coma. The world does not need more lethal weapons, larger armies, use of bots (robots), nanotechnology designed weaponry, artificial intelligence or microchipped humans but spiritually transformed individuals! As more and more individuals are transformed by God into compassionate, merciful and loving persons society will change for the better. This transformation process must reach critical mass point to usher in a paradigm (archetype) shift. We have invested human beings with too much power for too long with devastating consequences. We dare not continue doing so.

The Beloved interacts with individuals i.e. He sent Gabriel to personally encounter Mary. He yearns for a one-to-one relationship with each person. Our Creator IS compassionate, loving and tender. We place too much trust in humans and not enough in Him. People have always laughed, scoffed and quipped, "Where is God?" and mocked those they thought puerile for believing in a Supreme Being. People are still laughing, mockingly and jokingly today and asking, "Where is God?" They forget that a thousand years is as one day to God!

Breaking News! The angels announced the following message to the shepherds when Jesus was born:

"Be not afraid; for behold, I bring you GOOD NEWS of a GREAT JOY which will come to ALL the people; for to you is born THIS DAY in the city of David a SAVIOUR, who is Christ the Lord."

"And suddenly there was with the angels a multitude of heavenly host praising God and saying, "Glory to God in the highest, and on earth peace among men with whom he is pleased!" "Be not afraid!"

It's almost identical to the message Archangel Gabriel delivered to Mary! God doesn't desire us to fear Him! Why do we and why should we fear God? Strange that we fear God yet we trust man! If God doesn't exist – then, there is nothing! Life is then reduced to a dead-end road. BUT, God is a reality and God does exist. He is the Ultimate Reality.

ISAIAH Ch.52 verse 7

How beautiful upon the mountains are the feet of him who bring good tidings,
Who publishes peace, which brings good tiding of good?
Who publishes salvation?

We desperately need beautiful feet that bring good news, who publish peace, that carry wonderful and inspiring news! How we need publishers who publish salvation i.e. news that recues and saves! How urgently our parched, flagellated earth needs people to be conduits (channels) for good news.

Breaking News!

In the Beloved, we have everything - without God we are nothing! Life is uncertain, however, this is certain - NOTHING can or will separate us from God. We can bet our last dollar on this divine promise. Man and all the principalities –seen or unseen, are powerless to alter this divine decree. We are NEVER alone. Our Beloved is with us all ways and always!

When the physical body dies, we will be alive in Him. Our "dead" loved ones are not in a grave or an urn but safe and secure with God. Where they are is no more pain, fear, torment, suffering, darkness or loneliness. Life can no longer hurt or frighten them for it no longer has power over them. We WILL be re-united with our loved ones. Jesus has gone ahead to prepare a place for us and that place will include our loved ones.

Let's become co-creators with God. He is the Ultimate Creator and has given us the privilege to co-create with Him. Be His agent on earth and a bearer of good news that will lighten loads and bring a song to hearts. In small ways we can make big differences. The Alchemist transforms ashes into beauty and mourning into song. He longs to transfigure our ashes into something beautiful and transmute our mourning lament into a joyous song. I am tired of ugliness and filth. Trash seems to be everywhere: in movies, songs, language, the way we treat each other and the dumped garbage that blights landscapes. The illegal dumping of junk and litter is becoming a huge problem. People casually dump their trash on convenient sites which costs the council millions annually in disposal expenditure. There is also too much dumping of mental and emotional garbage via movies, television, lyrics and foul language. This reveals disdain and disrespect for audience and is barbaric! Someone creates the toxic trash (rubbish) and then dumps it onto audiences under the dubious title of entertainment or art. Why do we tolerate this? Why don't we stand up to this kind of abuse by turning our backs on it and its creators?

I want to plant a beautiful garden wherever I go where bees, butterflies and birds are welcome. The Beloved gifted us with a magnificent garden but, more's the pity, we abused and neglected it. It may be salvaged but it is going to require will, desire and effort on a world-wide scale if it is to be reinstated to what it was intended.

Hear the Christmas story as if for the first time! Imagination is required. Visualize the following scene: switch on the television set and see a flashing BREAKING NEWS sign - Jesus, Son of God, was born today in Bethlehem in a manger to a local couple Mary and Joseph. Magi from the East brought gifts of gold, myrrh and frankincense to the baby. They had travelled a long way following a star! This star showed the way to the Super Star in Bethlehem. Shepherds in nearby fields reported that angels appeared and reported that the birth of Jesus was a great and joyous event on earth and in heaven and that He came from God as an expression of His love. The shepherds were told to report the message to this station and it is now being broadcast throughout the world.

Coo'ee My dear child,

I have breaking news for you. It's not really new news at all! I love you and I have never stopped loving you…….and never will stop loving you.

I want you to co-operate with Me and be My fellow-creator. There is a great amount of work to be done and I require workers. You have so much potential and many gifts – use them in My service. If you let them atrophy; you add to the world's woes and troubles. They aren't yours to do with as you will. I entrusted them to you and expect you to use and multiply and magnify them. The world needs you.

I wish to use you as an instrument of peace and a conduit of beauty and healing. Plant gardens in minds and hearts. Work in unison with Me. Withdraw from the world and recharge your spiritual batteries. Speak to Me. I hear you. I speak to you. When you are re-charged, go back to the world and be a bearer of messages of good cheer. Be swift in conveying the joyful messages of hope and healing. Be an oasis and let the weary and thirsty find comfort in Me through you. Go in peace and know I go with you – always!

CHAPTER SEVENTEEN

RSVP
REPONDEZ S'IL VOUS PLAIT
– PLEASE ANSWER

I wish to conclude this book with a few "Come's". Come means to start, or move, or be brought towards. It is an invitation. The Beloved is an Initiator who gets things started and moving. He draws people towards Him as a magnet draws iron filings. Genesis Ch. 1:1 "IN THE BEGINNING…. GOD" - The First Mover/Starter/Initiator. After Adam and Eve disobeyed God, they hid, moved away and put distance between them and Him. They initiated their own downfall. God didn't wash his hands off them. He sought them and moved towards them in their hiding place. He called, "Where are you?" God is omniscient and knew what they had done, why they were hiding and where they were hiding. He invited them to come into the open, own up and take responsibility for their deeds. They didn't. "Where are you?" rings down the ages to us today and asks us to reply. It would be wise for us to consider where we are in our relationship with God, self, with people and the planet. Why are we running from God? What are we using as camouflage to avoid an encounter with God? Just why are we running and hiding? I must ask myself these questions too.

I received an invitation requesting my presence at a birthday supper which was to be held in a castle, situated on an island. My name was handwritten on the envelope. The venue, date, time were printed on the card and at the bottom, in small print, were the letters RVSP, an email address, mobile number and the latest date by which to accept or decline the invitation. I accepted and complied with the request to respondéz s'il vous plait!

We live in an age of entitlement wherein people feel entitled to all manner of things and is carried-over into relationships. Love is not an entitlement. I recently heard a teenager say, "My parents owe me. I didn't ask to be born or to be their son!" Love can't be bribed, coerced, manipulated, forced or owed. Some people say, "If you really love me, you would ….." That's trickery and bribery. Love is a GIFT. A true lover is a giver. Generosity and love are co-joined. Entitlement is selfish, immature, narcissistic and ego-inflated. Someone who feels entitled is a selfish grabber, taker, grasper and abuser.

I was humbled by the invitation. The person had sought me out and moved towards me through the invitation. She could have excluded me. It was her birthday and her choice whom to invite. I wasn't always so appreciative. I wasn't wise when I was younger and firmly believed my family was obligated to me. As for my friends, they simply had to invite me and when they didn't, I sulked and threw tantrums. How dare they not include me! Oh yes, I was a spoilt brat who demanded consideration and entitled to inclusion. My dad, mom and brothers simply HAD to love me – end of story! But, thankfully, I outgrew my childishness.

The ego is at the center of entitlement. An inflated ego considers itself of supreme importance and expects to be preened and pampered by others. People have every right to include or exclude whomsoever they wish to include or exclude at their functions and events as financial constraints are a factor. Many a person is in debt by trying not to offend anyone.

It is obvious that it is no longer considered necessary to respond to an invitation. A friend sent out numerous invitations to parents of children her son wished to attend his birthday party. He was only seven years old. They were posted or hand-delivered. She received one reply - ONE! Undaunted, she booked the venue and ordered catering for thirty children for, as she said, "People are so busy these days they probably forgot to reply so I catered for thirty - just in case!" Two children attended the party - TWO!!! Paul was inconsolable and couldn't understand why his friends never came. Spare a thought also for mom and dad who had to fork out for the excess catering and the hiring of a hall. Not replying to the invitation was rude, lazy and inexcusable! Entitlement is a bad personality flaw and shows itself through bad manners, impoliteness and thoughtless. Is this the norm? Our children observe and model our behavior and that, in part, explains the deplorable lack of politeness, manners and thoughtlessness that is evident and prevalent in society today.

Some behavior is beyond decency. Some non-invited thugs "crash" parties. Total strangers barge in and hijack the event. They come - uninvited and unwelcome and proceed to eat the food, drink the drink and behave in such disgusting ways that it ruins the evening for the invited guests and hosts. These buffoons consider it fun to raid somebody's special occasion! They feel entitled to do as they please. They are immature, boorish, self-centered, and barbaric and their actions are deplorable, childish and inexcusable.

God invites us to enter into a relationship with Him. A wedding is a happy, joyous event and so too should a relationship with Him be joyous and happy. The Beloved has invited us to come to Him. He sought Adam and Eve until He found them and He is searching for us. God is the mover – the relentless initiator. Are we searching for Him, or, like Adam and Eve did, run away and hiding from Him? We are not entitled to God or a relationship with Him. He owes us nothing. The Beloved seeks and searches because of His capacity to love – not because we are lovable and entitled to it. Grace smashes to smithereens the notion of entitlement!

The Almighty is patient and long-suffering. Did the world go hysterical with joy when Jesus was born? It did not. For thirty-three years He was misunderstood and maligned. The human race showed its lack of gratitude for God's Gift by rejecting, torturing and crucifying Jesus! The crucifixion was the work of man - the resurrection was the work of God.

I watched the Olympic Games that were held in Rio de Janeiro, Brazil. People were amazed when Usain Bolt won race after race. Why aren't people amazed and excited regarding God and His feats? Why don't they cheer Him? Why don't we stand up and sing when we realize who Jesus is and what He accomplished? People bayed for Jesus's blood when Pontius Pilate asked the crowd what he should do with Him,

"Shall I release Him or Barabbas?"

They shouted, hysterically, over and over again,

"Crucify Him. Crucify Him!" they jeered.

Pilate granted them their request. Jesus was whipped, mocked and crucified. The masses dispersed when He dismissed His spirit. They thought that was the end of the story - Jesus was dead and buried in a borrowed tomb. HOWEVER, three days later He returned neither dead nor gone! He remained on earth for a while and showed Himself and His wounded body to the disbelievers. One of His disciples thought it too good to be true and required proof. Jesus obliged by standing before Thomas and requested him to put his fingers into His wounds. As Thomas trembled in front of Him, He told him and the other disciples not to be afraid. No Olympic Games feat ever bettered that! Jesus didn't have a gold medal draped over His shoulders in acknowledgment of His amazing feats nor was He applauded by an ecstatic, appreciative crowd. No matter - He was elevated higher than any Olympic athlete by God. Millions upon millions of angels and the inhabitants of all the spheres and dimensions applauded His accomplishment. Jesus defeated death. He was and is the most evolved soul ever to walk on and grace earth.

What does God see in us? Why does He consider us when we are so often like truant, ungrateful rascals? We squander the earth's resources, our opportunities, potential, gifts, health and life and live as if we will never die. We aren't immortal or invincible. Whether we like it or not - we will all die. We are the ones who need God. So, why does God put-up with us? We certainly haven't endeared ourselves to Him. In mercy and compassion, He remembers that we are oh-so fragile. We are like the grass that takes root, briefly flourishes, withers and dies. He is cognizant that life on earth is precarious, strewn with troubles, woes, and uncertainties and interspersed with sprinklings of joy and happiness. The Father understands and is merciful and compassionate. We are pitiful in our pathetic self-imposed independence and our make-believe acts of self-importance! Oh, how we need God!

God is love. We are not in our right mind when we reject Love (God). There is something radically wrong when we declare our independence - our personal God-exist. When we do, it is like the earth declining the light and warmth of the sun in order to venture alone into the dark abyss.

The Wonderful, Wondrous Father invites us to come to Him. An invitation is half a transaction. The rainbow, seen from below the sky, is half a rainbow. When viewed from the sky, it is a complete rainbow. The Beloved has done His part but the invitation is incomplete without a reply or response. How can we ignore God's reaching out to us or treat His patience and kindness with disdain? He has invited us and He is awaiting our response/ reply.

Jesus said:

"It is finished."

It means -

"My mission on earth is accomplished. My work is complete!"

Softly and tenderly God is coo'ing to you. He is inviting you to newness of life, heart, attitude, spirit - new beginning and a new you.

2 CORINTHIANS 5:17: "Therefore, if anyone is in Christ, he is a new creature; the old has gone, the new has come!"

PLEASE ANSWER – REPONDEZ'IL VOUS PLAIT

Coo'ee My dear, dear one,

I am inviting you to My banquet. Please come. I have prepared everything.

I stand at the portals and wait. I knock on your door. I come to you.

Never be afraid of Me. I love you and wish to lavish My gifts on you for I am generous and kind.

No banquet on earth can or will match My banquet. I want you to enjoy life but I don't want you to indulge yourself in things that leave you empty and broken.

Your mind cannot comprehend My love and neither can you imagine what awaits you when your time arrives for you to come Home.

Fear not My little one for I AM with you. There is no power, no principality or anything seen and unseen, known or unknown that can separate you from Me. Life can't and death won't. No matter where you go – even if you go to mars, you cannot go beyond Me. I AM. I AM. I AM.

Invite Me into your heart and life - I WILL answer. I AM at the door of your heart and I AM knocking. Can you hear the knocking? Open the door. I will open a door to you that nothing and nobody can shut.

As a bird returns to its nest, return to ME.

REVELATIONS 22:20

"Surely I am coming soon"
Amen. Come Lord Jesus!

MARANATHA!

REFERENCES
THE REVISED STANDARD VERSION.
PUBLISHED BY WILLIAM
COLLINS SONS AND CO. LTD.

CHAPTER ONE
Genesis 1:28-31

CHAPTER TWO
Genesis 3:13-14
Hebrews 13:5

CHAPTER THREE
Genesis 20:4, Genesis 32:1-4
Genesis 3:13-14
Genesis 2:7
Psalm 139
Exodus 3:5

CHAPTER FOUR
Matthew 26:36-46
Matthew 11:28
Hebrews 13:5

CHAPTER FIVE
Matthew 11:28
Psalm 46:10
Jeremiah 2:13, John 4:10
Isaiah 41:10 + vs. 13

CHAPTER SIX
Luke 10:29-37
Matthew 6:16-18
Genesis 3:9-13
Exodus 3:1314
Psalm 139
Matthew 23:37
Matthew 11:28

CHAPTER SEVEN
Genesis 1:29-31
Genesis 5:2
2 Peter 2:8
John 3:16
Exodus 3:13-14
Psalm 46:10
Genesis 11:3-8

CHAPTER EIGHT
Matthew 26:57, Matthew 13-26
Exodus 32:1-4
Exodus 20:1-17
Exodus 14:10-12, Ch.16:2-3
Genesis 1:1
1 John 4:7-8
Revelations 16:16
Genesis 3:23-24
Luke 1:11 (Numerous references to angels)
John 10:30
John 3:16
Exodus: 3:5
Revelations 3:20
Genesis 2:16-17, Genesis 3:6
Hebrews 11:5
Matthew 11:28

CHAPTER NINE
Luke 2:8-13
1 John 4:7-8
Exodus 16:13-19
Exodus 20:4-17
Genesis 3:9-10
2 Corinthians 3:2
Romans 3:23
Luke 15:11-24
Psalm 90:2
Lamentations 3:21-23
Hebrews 3:7-8
1 Kings 18:20-46, 1 Kings 19:1-16
1 Kings 19:12
Deuteronomy 33:27

CHAPTER TEN
1 Kings 17:2-6
Psalm 17:8
Psalm 139, Romans 8:37-39
Mark 16:19, Luke 24:5-52

CHAPTER ELEVEN
Poem by Percy Shelley - "Ozymandias"
Revelations 3:20
Matthew 7:7-8

CHAPTER TWELVE:
Matthew 6:25-27
John 14:6
Genesis 2:15-17
Genesis 3:8-12
John 14:6
John 18:28-40, John 19, John 20
Matthew 3:13-17
Matthew 27:45-46

Luke 2:1-7
Luke 1:26-38, 46-47
Mark 16:1-13, 16:19-20
1 Corinthians 15:51-55
Genesis 3:8-12

CHAPTER THIRTEEN
1 Kings19:1-18
Hebrews 3:7-8
Leviticus 11:45, 1 Samuel 2:2, Revelations 4:8
Genesis 4:1-10
John 14:6
Matthew 21:18-22
John 8:44-45
Genesis 2:16
Matthew 12:33
John 14:2
John 14:6
Genesis 3:8-9
Hebrews 1:14
Luke 2:8-14
Luke 2:8-15
John 20:11-13
Luke 1:26-31
Isaiah 55:3, Jeremiah 7:22-24, 2 Chronicles 7:14
John 1:14, Psalm 117:2
1 John 1:5-10, Numbers 23:19
Genesis 2:16, 3:1-12
Matthew 16:26

CHAPTER FOURTEEN
William Shakespeare – Macbeth
Matthew 27:24-26
1 John 1:8-10, Romans 3:23
Isaiah 41:9-10
Matthew 23:5-7, Matthew 23:13-34

Matthew 12:1-8
Mark 2:27
Isaiah 1:10-16, Psalm 51:16-17
Genesis 2:8-12
Genesis 1:16-17, Genesis 3:6
2 Samuel 11:2-17
Psalm 51:1-17
Genesis 4:8-10
Psalm 51:1-17
Psalm 51:16
Ephesians 2:4-5
Psalm 51:17
Isaiah 1:18
Psalm 51:17
Romans 3:23
Psalm 103:14
Revelations 3:7, Rev 4:1
Revelations 3:20:

CHAPTER FIFTEEN
Genesis 1:1-3,
Job 11:7-8,
Job 38:4-4
Genesis 1:1-3,
Numbers 22:21-35
Genesis 2:15
The Book of Tobit – The Apocryphal: Catholic Bible
Luke 1:26-35
Acts 8:26-40
Mark 16:1-8
Luke 24:9-12
John 20:11-18
Isaiah 49:15-16, Deuteronomy: 33:26-27, Jeremiah 31:3
Matthew 25:14-29
Genesis 3:1-6
Hebrews 13:5

CHAPTER SIXTEEN
Jonah 1
Genesis 19:15-29
Genesis 19:26
Genesis 12:1
Exodus 5:1
Luke 1:26-38
Luke 1:30
Luke 1:38
Matthew 11:14-15, Hebrews 3:7-8
1 Corinthians 7:23
Genesis 7:1-7
Luke 1: 26-38
Matthew 2:8-15
Hebrews 13:5
Genesis 2:15

CHAPTER SEVENTEEN
Genesis 1:1-2
Matthew 11:29

Genesis 3:9
Genesis 3:10
Matthew 27:15-24
John 15:16-17
1 John 4:7-8
John 19:30
Exodus 3:14
Revelations 3:20

Printed in the United States
By Bookmasters